INDONESIAN
V O C A B U L A R Y

FOR ENGLISH SPEAKERS

ENGLISH-
INDONESIAN

The most useful words
To expand your lexicon and sharpen
your language skills

3000 words

Indonesian vocabulary for English speakers - 3000 words

By Andrey Taranov

T&P Books vocabularies are intended for helping you learn, memorize and review foreign words. The dictionary is divided into themes, covering all major spheres of everyday activities, business, science, culture, etc.

The process of learning words using T&P Books' theme-based dictionaries gives you the following advantages:

- Correctly grouped source information predetermines success at subsequent stages of word memorization
- Availability of words derived from the same root allowing memorization of word units (rather than separate words)
- Small units of words facilitate the process of establishing associative links needed for consolidation of vocabulary
- Level of language knowledge can be estimated by the number of learned words

T&P Books Publishing
www.tpbooks.com

ISBN: 978-1-78616-483-4

This book is also available in E-book formats.
Please visit www.tpbooks.com or the major online bookstores.

INDONESIAN VOCABULARY
for English speakers

T&P Books vocabularies are intended to help you learn, memorize, and review foreign words. The vocabulary contains over 3000 commonly used words arranged thematically.

- Vocabulary contains the most commonly used words
- Recommended as an addition to any language course
- Meets the needs of beginners and advanced learners of foreign languages
- Convenient for daily use, revision sessions, and self-testing activities
- Allows you to assess your vocabulary

Special features of the vocabulary

- Words are organized according to their meaning, not alphabetically
- Words are presented in three columns to facilitate the reviewing and self-testing processes
- Words in groups are divided into small blocks to facilitate the learning process
- The vocabulary offers a convenient and simple transcription of each foreign word

The vocabulary has 101 topics including:

Basic Concepts, Numbers, Colors, Months, Seasons, Units of Measurement, Clothing & Accessories, Food & Nutrition, Restaurant, Family Members, Relatives, Character, Feelings, Emotions, Diseases, City, Town, Sightseeing, Shopping, Money, House, Home, Office, Working in the Office, Import & Export, Marketing, Job Search, Sports, Education, Computer, Internet, Tools, Nature, Countries, Nationalities and more ...

T&P BOOKS' THEME-BASED DICTIONARIES

The Correct System for Memorizing Foreign Words

Acquiring vocabulary is one of the most important elements of learning a foreign language, because words allow us to express our thoughts, ask questions, and provide answers. An inadequate vocabulary can impede communication with a foreigner and make it difficult to understand a book or movie well.

The pace of activity in all spheres of modern life, including the learning of modern languages, has increased. Today, we need to memorize large amounts of information (grammar rules, foreign words, etc.) within a short period. However, this does not need to be difficult. All you need to do is to choose the right training materials, learn a few special techniques, and develop your individual training system.

Having a system is critical to the process of language learning. Many people fail to succeed in this regard; they cannot master a foreign language because they fail to follow a system comprised of selecting materials, organizing lessons, arranging new words to be learned, and so on. The lack of a system causes confusion and eventually, lowers self-confidence.

T&P Books' theme-based dictionaries can be included in the list of elements needed for creating an effective system for learning foreign words. These dictionaries were specially developed for learning purposes and are meant to help students effectively memorize words and expand their vocabulary.

Generally speaking, the process of learning words consists of three main elements:

- Reception (creation or acquisition) of a training material, such as a word list
- Work aimed at memorizing new words
- Work aimed at reviewing the learned words, such as self-testing

All three elements are equally important since they determine the quality of work and the final result. All three processes require certain skills and a well-thought-out approach.

New words are often encountered quite randomly when learning a foreign language and it may be difficult to include them all in a unified list. As a result, these words remain written on scraps of paper, in book margins, textbooks, and so on. In order to systematize such words, we have to create and continually update a "book of new words." A paper notebook, a netbook, or a tablet PC can be used for these purposes.

This "book of new words" will be your personal, unique list of words. However, it will only contain the words that you came across during the learning process. For example, you might have written down the words "Sunday," "Tuesday," and "Friday." However, there are additional words for days of the week, for example, "Saturday," that are missing, and your list of words would be incomplete. Using a theme dictionary, in addition to the "book of new words," is a reasonable solution to this problem.

The theme-based dictionary may serve as the basis for expanding your vocabulary.

It will be your big "book of new words" containing the most frequently used words of a foreign language already included. There are quite a few theme-based dictionaries available, and you should ensure that you make the right choice in order to get the maximum benefit from your purchase.

Therefore, we suggest using theme-based dictionaries from T&P Books Publishing as an aid to learning foreign words. Our books are specially developed for effective use in the sphere of vocabulary systematization, expansion and review.

Theme-based dictionaries are not a magical solution to learning new words. However, they can serve as your main database to aid foreign-language acquisition. Apart from theme dictionaries, you can have copybooks for writing down new words, flash cards, glossaries for various texts, as well as other resources; however, a good theme dictionary will always remain your primary collection of words.

T&P Books' theme-based dictionaries are specialty books that contain the most frequently used words in a language.

The main characteristic of such dictionaries is the division of words into themes. For example, the *City* theme contains the words "street," "crossroads," "square," "fountain," and so on. The *Talking* theme might contain words like "to talk," "to ask," "question," and "answer".

All the words in a theme are divided into smaller units, each comprising 3–5 words. Such an arrangement improves the perception of words and makes the learning process less tiresome. Each unit contains a selection of words with similar meanings or identical roots. This allows you to learn words in small groups and establish other associative links that have a positive effect on memorization.

The words on each page are placed in three columns: a word in your native language, its translation, and its transcription. Such positioning allows for the use of techniques for effective memorization. After closing the translation column, you can flip through and review foreign words, and vice versa. "This is an easy and convenient method of review – one that we recommend you do often."

Our theme-based dictionaries contain transcriptions for all the foreign words. Unfortunately, none of the existing transcriptions are able to convey the exact nuances of foreign pronunciation. That is why we recommend using the transcriptions only as a supplementary learning aid. Correct pronunciation can only be acquired with the help of sound. Therefore our collection includes audio theme-based dictionaries.

The process of learning words using T&P Books' theme-based dictionaries gives you the following advantages:

- You have correctly grouped source information, which predetermines your success at subsequent stages of word memorization
- Availability of words derived from the same root (lazy, lazily, lazybones), allowing you to memorize word units instead of separate words
- Small units of words facilitate the process of establishing associative links needed for consolidation of vocabulary
- You can estimate the number of learned words and hence your level of language knowledge
- The dictionary allows for the creation of an effective and high-quality revision process
- You can revise certain themes several times, modifying the revision methods and techniques
- Audio versions of the dictionaries help you to work out the pronunciation of words and develop your skills of auditory word perception

The T&P Books' theme-based dictionaries are offered in several variants differing in the number of words: 1.500, 3.000, 5.000, 7.000, and 9.000 words. There are also dictionaries containing 15,000 words for some language combinations. Your choice of dictionary will depend on your knowledge level and goals.

We sincerely believe that our dictionaries will become your trusty assistant in learning foreign languages and will allow you to easily acquire the necessary vocabulary.

TABLE OF CONTENTS

PRONUNCIATION GUIDE

Letter	Indonesian example	T&P phonetic alphabet	English example
Aa	zaman	[a]	shorter than in ask
Bb	besar	[b]	baby, book
Cc	kecil, cepat	[ʧ]	church, French
Dd	dugaan	[d]	day, doctor
Ee	segera, mencium	[e], [ə]	medal, elm
Ff	berfungsi	[f]	face, food
Gg	juga, lagi	[g]	game, gold
Hh	hanya, bahwa	[h]	home, have
Ii	izin, sebagai ganti	[i], [j]	Peter, yard
Jj	setuju, ijin	[ʤ]	jeans, gin
Kk	kemudian, tidak	[k], [ʔ]	kiss, glottal stop
Ll	dilarang	[l]	lace, people
Mm	melihat	[m]	magic, milk
Nn	berenang	[n], [ŋ]	name, ring
Oo	toko roti	[o:]	fall, bomb
Pp	peribahasa	[p]	pencil, private
Qq	Aquarius	[k]	clock, kiss
Rr	ratu, riang	[r]	trilled [r]
Ss	sendok, syarat	[s], [ʃ]	city, machine
Tt	tamu, adat	[t]	tourist, trip
Uu	ambulans	[u]	book
Vv	renovasi	[v]	very, river
Ww	pariwisata	[w]	vase, winter
Xx	boxer	[ks]	box, taxi
Yy	banyak, syarat	[j]	yes, New York
Zz	zamrud	[z]	zebra, please

Combinations of letters

aa	maaf	[aʔa]	a+glottal stop
kh	khawatir	[h]	home, have
th	Gereja Lutheran	[t]	tourist, trip
-k	tidak	[ʔ]	glottal stop

ABBREVIATIONS
used in the vocabulary

English abbreviations

ab.	-	about
adj	-	adjective
adv	-	adverb
anim.	-	animate
as adj	-	attributive noun used as adjective
e.g.	-	for example
etc.	-	et cetera
fam.	-	familiar
fem.	-	feminine
form.	-	formal
inanim.	-	inanimate
masc.	-	masculine
math	-	mathematics
mil.	-	military
n	-	noun
pl	-	plural
pron.	-	pronoun
sb	-	somebody
sing.	-	singular
sth	-	something
v aux	-	auxiliary verb
vi	-	intransitive verb
vi, vt	-	intransitive, transitive verb
vt	-	transitive verb

BASIC CONCEPTS

1. Pronouns

I, me	saya, aku	[saja], [aku]
you	engkau, kamu	[eŋkau], [kamu]
he, she, it	beliau, dia, ia	[beliau], [dia], [ia]
we	kami, kita	[kami], [kita]
you (to a group)	kalian	[kalian]
you (polite, sing.)	Anda	[anda]
you (polite, pl)	Anda sekalian	[anda sekalian]
they	mereka	[mereka]

2. Greetings. Salutations

Hello! (fam.)	Halo!	[halo!]
Hello! (form.)	Halo!	[halo!]
Good morning!	Selamat pagi!	[slamat pagi!]
Good afternoon!	Selamat siang!	[slamat siaŋ!]
Good evening!	Selamat sore!	[slamat sore!]
to say hello	menyapa	[mənjapa]
Hi! (hello)	Hai!	[hey!]
greeting (n)	sambutan, salam	[sambutan], [salam]
to greet (vt)	menyambut	[mənjambut]
How are you?	Apa kabar?	[apa kabar?]
What's new?	Apa yang baru?	[apa yaŋ baru?]
Goodbye! (form.)	Selamat tinggal! Selamat jalan!	[slamat tiŋgal!], [slamat dʒʲalan!]
Bye! (fam.)	Dadah!	[dadah!]
See you soon!	Sampai bertemu lagi!	[sampaj bərtemu lagi!]
Farewell! (to a friend)	Sampai jumpa!	[sampaj dʒʲumpa!]
Farewell! (form.)	Selamat tinggal!	[slamat tiŋgal!]
to say goodbye	berpamitan	[bərpamitan]
So long!	Sampai nanti!	[sampaj nanti!]
Thank you!	Terima kasih!	[tərima kasih!]
Thank you very much!	Terima kasih banyak!	[tərima kasih banjaʔ!]
You're welcome	Kembali! Sama-sama!	[kembali!], [sama-sama!]
Don't mention it!	Kembali!	[kembali!]
It was nothing	Kembali!	[kembali!]
Excuse me! (apology)	Maaf, ...	[maʔaf, ...]

to excuse (forgive)	**memaafkan**	[mema'afkan]
to apologize (vi)	**meminta maaf**	[meminta ma'af]
My apologies	**Maafkan saya**	[ma'afkan saja]
I'm sorry!	**Maaf!**	[ma'af!]
to forgive (vt)	**memaafkan**	[mema'afkan]
It's okay! (that's all right)	**Tidak apa-apa!**	[tida' apa-apa!]
please (adv)	**tolong**	[toloŋ]
Don't forget!	**Jangan lupa!**	[dʒaŋan lupa!]
Certainly!	**Tentu!**	[tentu!]
Of course not!	**Tentu tidak!**	[tentu tida'!]
Okay! (I agree)	**Baiklah! Baik!**	[bajklah!], [baj'!]
That's enough!	**Cukuplah!**	[tʃukuplah!]

3. Questions

Who?	**Siapa?**	[siapa?]
What?	**Apa?**	[apa?]
Where? (at, in)	**Di mana?**	[di mana?]
Where (to)?	**Ke mana?**	[ke mana?]
From where?	**Dari mana?**	[dari mana?]
When?	**Kapan?**	[kapan?]
Why? (What for?)	**Mengapa?**	[meŋapa?]
Why? (~ are you crying?)	**Mengapa?**	[meŋapa?]
What for?	**Untuk apa?**	[untu' apa?]
How? (in what way)	**Bagaimana?**	[bagajmana?]
What? (What kind of ...?)	**Apa? Yang mana?**	[apa?], [yaŋ mana?]
Which?	**Yang mana?**	[yaŋ mana?]
To whom?	**Kepada siapa? Untuk siapa?**	[kepada siapa?], [untu' siapa?]
About whom?	**Tentang siapa?**	[tentaŋ siapa?]
About what?	**Tentang apa?**	[tentaŋ apa?]
With whom?	**Dengan siapa?**	[deŋan siapa?]
How many? How much?	**Berapa?**	[berapa?]
Whose?	**Milik siapa?**	[mili' siapa?]

4. Prepositions

with (accompanied by)	**dengan**	[deŋan]
without	**tanpa**	[tanpa]
to (indicating direction)	**ke**	[ke]
about (talking ~ ...)	**tentang ...**	[tentaŋ ...]
before (in time)	**sebelum**	[sebelum]
in front of ...	**di depan ...**	[di depan ...]
under (beneath, below)	**di bawah**	[di bawah]

above (over)	di atas	[di atas]
on (atop)	di atas	[di atas]
from (off, out of)	dari	[dari]
of (made from)	dari	[dari]

| in (e.g., ~ ten minutes) | dalam | [dalam] |
| over (across the top of) | melalui | [melalui] |

5. Function words. Adverbs. Part 1

Where? (at, in)	Di mana?	[di mana?]
here (adv)	di sini	[di sini]
there (adv)	di sana	[di sana]

| somewhere (to be) | di suatu tempat | [di suatu tempat] |
| nowhere (not anywhere) | tak ada di mana pun | [ta' ada di mana pun] |

| by (near, beside) | dekat | [dekat] |
| by the window | dekat jendela | [dekat dʒʲendela] |

Where (to)?	Ke mana?	[ke mana?]
here (e.g., come ~!)	ke sini	[ke sini]
there (e.g., to go ~)	ke sana	[ke sana]
from here (adv)	dari sini	[dari sini]
from there (adv)	dari sana	[dari sana]

| close (adv) | dekat | [dekat] |
| far (adv) | jauh | [dʒʲauh] |

near (e.g., ~ Paris)	dekat	[dekat]
nearby (adv)	dekat	[dekat]
not far (adv)	tidak jauh	[tida' dʒʲauh]

left (adj)	kiri	[kiri]
on the left	di kiri	[di kiri]
to the left	ke kiri	[ke kiri]

right (adj)	kanan	[kanan]
on the right	di kanan	[di kanan]
to the right	ke kanan	[ke kanan]

in front (adv)	di depan	[di depan]
front (as adj)	depan	[depan]
ahead (the kids ran ~)	ke depan	[ke depan]

behind (adv)	di belakang	[di belakaŋ]
from behind	dari belakang	[dari belakaŋ]
back (towards the rear)	mundur	[mundur]
middle	tengah	[teŋah]
in the middle	di tengah	[di teŋah]

at the side	di sisi, di samping	[di sisi], [di sampiŋ]
everywhere (adv)	di mana-mana	[di mana-mana]
around (in all directions)	di sekitar	[di sekitar]

from inside	dari dalam	[dari dalam]
somewhere (to go)	ke suatu tempat	[ke suatu tempat]
straight (directly)	terus	[terus]
back (e.g., come ~)	kembali	[kembali]

| from anywhere | dari mana pun | [dari mana pun] |
| from somewhere | dari suatu tempat | [dari suatu tempat] |

firstly (adv)	pertama	[pərtama]
secondly (adv)	kedua	[kedua]
thirdly (adv)	ketiga	[ketiga]

suddenly (adv)	tiba-tiba	[tiba-tiba]
at first (in the beginning)	mula-mula	[mula-mula]
for the first time	untuk pertama kalinya	[untu' pertama kalinja]
long before …	jauh sebelum …	[dʒ'auh sebelum …]
anew (over again)	kembali	[kembali]
for good (adv)	untuk selama-lamanya	[untu' selama-lamanja]

never (adv)	tidak pernah	[tida' pərnah]
again (adv)	lagi, kembali	[lagi], [kembali]
now (adv)	sekarang	[sekaraŋ]
often (adv)	sering, seringkali	[seriŋ], [seriŋkali]
then (adv)	ketika itu	[ketika itu]
urgently (quickly)	segera	[segera]
usually (adv)	biasanya	[biasanja]

by the way, …	ngomong-ngomong …	[ŋomoŋ-ŋomoŋ …]
possible (that is ~)	mungkin	[muŋkin]
probably (adv)	mungkin	[muŋkin]
maybe (adv)	mungkin	[muŋkin]
besides …	selain itu …	[selajn itu …]
that's why …	karena itu …	[karena itu …]
in spite of …	meskipun …	[meskipun …]
thanks to …	berkat …	[berkat …]

what (pron.)	apa	[apa]
that (conj.)	bahwa	[bahwa]
something	sesuatu	[sesuatu]
anything (something)	sesuatu	[sesuatu]
nothing	tidak sesuatu pun	[tida' sesuatu pun]

who (pron.)	siapa	[siapa]
someone	seseorang	[seseoraŋ]
somebody	seseorang	[seseoraŋ]

| nobody | tidak seorang pun | [tida' seoraŋ pun] |
| nowhere (a voyage to ~) | tidak ke mana pun | [tida' ke mana pun] |

nobody's	tidak milik siapa pun	[tidaʾ miliʾ siapa pun]
somebody's	milik seseorang	[miliʾ seseoraŋ]
so (I'm ~ glad)	sangat	[saŋat]
also (as well)	juga	[dʒʲuga]
too (as well)	juga	[dʒʲuga]

6. Function words. Adverbs. Part 2

Why?	Mengapa?	[məŋapa?]
for some reason	entah mengapa	[entah məŋapa]
because …	karena …	[karena …]
for some purpose	untuk tujuan tertentu	[untuʾ tudʒʲuan tərtentu]
and	dan	[dan]
or	atau	[atau]
but	tetapi, namun	[tetapi], [namun]
for (e.g., ~ me)	untuk	[untuʾ]
too (~ many people)	terlalu	[tərlalu]
only (exclusively)	hanya	[hanja]
exactly (adv)	tepat	[tepat]
about (more or less)	sekitar	[sekitar]
approximately (adv)	kira-kira	[kira-kira]
approximate (adj)	kira-kira	[kira-kira]
almost (adv)	hampir	[hampir]
the rest	selebihnya, sisanya	[selebihnja], [sisanja]
the other (second)	kedua	[kedua]
other (different)	lain	[lain]
each (adj)	setiap	[setiap]
any (no matter which)	sebarang	[sebaraŋ]
many, much (a lot of)	banyak	[banjaʾ]
many people	banyak orang	[banjaʾ oraŋ]
all (everyone)	semua	[semua]
in return for …	sebagai ganti …	[sebagaj ganti …]
in exchange (adv)	sebagai gantinya	[sebagaj gantinja]
by hand (made)	dengan tangan	[deŋan taŋan]
hardly (negative opinion)	hampir tidak	[hampir tidaʾ]
probably (adv)	mungkin	[muŋkin]
on purpose (intentionally)	sengaja	[seŋadʒʲa]
by accident (adv)	tidak sengaja	[tidaʾ seŋadʒʲa]
very (adv)	sangat	[saŋat]
for example (adv)	misalnya	[misalnja]
between	antara	[antara]
among	di antara	[di antara]

| so much (such a lot) | **banyak sekali** | [banja' sekali] |
| especially (adv) | **terutama** | [terutama] |

NUMBERS. MISCELLANEOUS

7. Cardinal numbers. Part 1

0 zero	**nol**	[nol]
1 one	**satu**	[satu]
2 two	**dua**	[dua]
3 three	**tiga**	[tiga]
4 four	**empat**	[empat]
5 five	**lima**	[lima]
6 six	**enam**	[enam]
7 seven	**tujuh**	[tudʒʲuh]
8 eight	**delapan**	[delapan]
9 nine	**sembilan**	[sembilan]
10 ten	**sepuluh**	[sepuluh]
11 eleven	**sebelas**	[sebelas]
12 twelve	**dua belas**	[dua belas]
13 thirteen	**tiga belas**	[tiga belas]
14 fourteen	**empat belas**	[empat belas]
15 fifteen	**lima belas**	[lima belas]
16 sixteen	**enam belas**	[enam belas]
17 seventeen	**tujuh belas**	[tudʒʲuh belas]
18 eighteen	**delapan belas**	[delapan belas]
19 nineteen	**sembilan belas**	[sembilan belas]
20 twenty	**dua puluh**	[dua puluh]
21 twenty-one	**dua puluh satu**	[dua puluh satu]
22 twenty-two	**dua puluh dua**	[dua puluh dua]
23 twenty-three	**dua puluh tiga**	[dua puluh tiga]
30 thirty	**tiga puluh**	[tiga puluh]
31 thirty-one	**tiga puluh satu**	[tiga puluh satu]
32 thirty-two	**tiga puluh dua**	[tiga puluh dua]
33 thirty-three	**tiga puluh tiga**	[tiga puluh tiga]
40 forty	**empat puluh**	[empat puluh]
41 forty-one	**empat puluh satu**	[empat puluh satu]
42 forty-two	**empat puluh dua**	[empat puluh dua]
43 forty-three	**empat puluh tiga**	[empat puluh tiga]
50 fifty	**lima puluh**	[lima puluh]
51 fifty-one	**lima puluh satu**	[lima puluh satu]
52 fifty-two	**lima puluh dua**	[lima puluh dua]

53 fifty-three	lima puluh tiga	[lima puluh tiga]
60 sixty	enam puluh	[enam puluh]
61 sixty-one	enam puluh satu	[enam puluh satu]
62 sixty-two	enam puluh dua	[enam puluh dua]
63 sixty-three	enam puluh tiga	[enam puluh tiga]
70 seventy	tujuh puluh	[tudʒʲuh puluh]
71 seventy-one	tujuh puluh satu	[tudʒʲuh puluh satu]
72 seventy-two	tujuh puluh dua	[tudʒʲuh puluh dua]
73 seventy-three	tujuh puluh tiga	[tudʒʲuh puluh tiga]
80 eighty	delapan puluh	[delapan puluh]
81 eighty-one	delapan puluh satu	[delapan puluh satu]
82 eighty-two	delapan puluh dua	[delapan puluh dua]
83 eighty-three	delapan puluh tiga	[delapan puluh tiga]
90 ninety	sembilan puluh	[sembilan puluh]
91 ninety-one	sembulan puluh satu	[sembulan puluh satu]
92 ninety-two	sembilan puluh dua	[sembilan puluh dua]
93 ninety-three	sembilan puluh tiga	[sembilan puluh tiga]

8. Cardinal numbers. Part 2

100 one hundred	seratus	[seratus]
200 two hundred	dua ratus	[dua ratus]
300 three hundred	tiga ratus	[tiga ratus]
400 four hundred	empat ratus	[empat ratus]
500 five hundred	lima ratus	[lima ratus]
600 six hundred	enam ratus	[enam ratus]
700 seven hundred	tujuh ratus	[tudʒʲuh ratus]
800 eight hundred	delapan ratus	[delapan ratus]
900 nine hundred	sembilan ratus	[sembilan ratus]
1000 one thousand	seribu	[seribu]
2000 two thousand	dua ribu	[dua ribu]
3000 three thousand	tiga ribu	[tiga ribu]
10000 ten thousand	sepuluh ribu	[sepuluh ribu]
one hundred thousand	seratus ribu	[seratus ribu]
million	juta	[dʒʲuta]
billion	miliar	[miliar]

9. Ordinal numbers

first (adj)	pertama	[pertama]
second (adj)	kedua	[kedua]
third (adj)	ketiga	[ketiga]
fourth (adj)	keempat	[keempat]

fifth (adj)	kelima	[kelima]
sixth (adj)	keenam	[keenam]
seventh (adj)	ketujuh	[ketudʒⁱuh]
eighth (adj)	kedelapan	[kedelapan]
ninth (adj)	kesembilan	[kesembilan]
tenth (adj)	kesepuluh	[kesepuluh]

COLOURS. UNITS OF MEASUREMENT

10. Colors

color	**warna**	[warna]
shade (tint)	**nuansa**	[nuansa]
hue	**warna**	[warna]
rainbow	**pelangi**	[pelaŋi]
white (adj)	**putih**	[putih]
black (adj)	**hitam**	[hitam]
gray (adj)	**kelabu**	[kelabu]
green (adj)	**hijau**	[hidʒʲau]
yellow (adj)	**kuning**	[kuniŋ]
red (adj)	**merah**	[merah]
blue (adj)	**biru**	[biru]
light blue (adj)	**biru muda**	[biru muda]
pink (adj)	**pink**	[pinʔ]
orange (adj)	**oranye, jingga**	[oranje], [dʒiŋga]
violet (adj)	**violet, ungu muda**	[violet], [uŋu muda]
brown (adj)	**cokelat**	[ʧokelat]
golden (adj)	**keemasan**	[keemasan]
silvery (adj)	**keperakan**	[keperakan]
beige (adj)	**abu-abu kecokelatan**	[abu-abu keʧokelatan]
cream (adj)	**krem**	[krem]
turquoise (adj)	**pirus**	[pirus]
cherry red (adj)	**merah tua**	[merah tua]
lilac (adj)	**ungu**	[uŋu]
crimson (adj)	**merah lembayung**	[merah lembajuŋ]
light (adj)	**terang**	[teraŋ]
dark (adj)	**gelap**	[gelap]
bright, vivid (adj)	**terang**	[teraŋ]
colored (pencils)	**berwarna**	[bərwarna]
color (e.g., ~ film)	**warna**	[warna]
black-and-white (adj)	**hitam-putih**	[hitam-putih]
plain (one-colored)	**polos, satu warna**	[polos], [satu warna]
multicolored (adj)	**berwarna-warni**	[bərwarna-warni]

11. Units of measurement

weight	berat	[berat]
length	panjang	[pandʒaŋ]
width	lebar	[lebar]
height	ketinggian	[ketiŋgian]
depth	kedalaman	[kedalaman]
volume	volume, isi	[volume], [isi]
area	luas	[luas]

gram	gram	[gram]
milligram	miligram	[miligram]
kilogram	kilogram	[kilogram]
ton	ton	[ton]
pound	pon	[pon]
ounce	ons	[ons]

meter	meter	[meter]
millimeter	milimeter	[milimeter]
centimeter	sentimeter	[sentimeter]
kilometer	kilometer	[kilometer]
mile	mil	[mil]

inch	inci	[intʃi]
foot	kaki	[kaki]
yard	yard	[yard]

square meter	meter persegi	[meter persegi]
hectare	hektar	[hektar]

liter	liter	[liter]
degree	derajat	[deradʒat]
volt	volt	[volt]
ampere	ampere	[ampere]
horsepower	tenaga kuda	[tenaga kuda]

quantity	kuantitas	[kuantitas]
a little bit of …	sedikit …	[sedikit …]
half	setengah	[seteŋah]

dozen	lusin	[lusin]
piece (item)	buah	[buah]

size	ukuran	[ukuran]
scale (map ~)	skala	[skala]

minimal (adj)	minimal	[minimal]
the smallest (adj)	terkecil	[terketʃil]
medium (adj)	sedang	[sedaŋ]
maximal (adj)	maksimal	[maksimal]
the largest (adj)	terbesar	[terbesar]

12. Containers

canning jar (glass ~)	**gelas**	[gelas]
can	**kaleng**	[kaleŋ]
bucket	**ember**	[ember]
barrel	**tong**	[toŋ]
wash basin (e.g., plastic ~)	**baskom**	[baskom]
tank (100L water ~)	**tangki**	[taŋki]
hip flask	**pelples**	[pelples]
jerrycan	**jeriken**	[dʒˈeriken]
tank (e.g., tank car)	**tangki**	[taŋki]
mug	**mangkuk**	[maŋkuʔ]
cup (of coffee, etc.)	**cangkir**	[ʧaŋkir]
saucer	**alas cangkir**	[alas ʧaŋkir]
glass (tumbler)	**gelas**	[gelas]
wine glass	**gelas anggur**	[gelas aŋgur]
stock pot (soup pot)	**panci**	[panʧi]
bottle (~ of wine)	**botol**	[botol]
neck (of the bottle, etc.)	**leher**	[leher]
carafe (decanter)	**karaf**	[karaf]
pitcher	**kendi**	[kendi]
vessel (container)	**wadah**	[wadah]
pot (crock, stoneware ~)	**pot**	[pot]
vase	**vas**	[vas]
bottle (perfume ~)	**botol**	[botol]
vial, small bottle	**botol kecil**	[botol keʧil]
tube (of toothpaste)	**tabung**	[tabuŋ]
sack (bag)	**karung**	[karuŋ]
bag (paper ~, plastic ~)	**kantong**	[kantoŋ]
pack (of cigarettes, etc.)	**bungkus**	[buŋkus]
box (e.g., shoebox)	**kotak, kardus**	[kotak], [kardus]
crate	**kotak**	[kotaʔ]
basket	**bakul**	[bakul]

MAIN VERBS

13. The most important verbs. Part 1

to advise (vt)	menasihati	[mənasihati]
to agree (say yes)	setuju	[setudʒiu]
to answer (vi, vt)	menjawab	[məndʒawab]
to apologize (vi)	meminta maaf	[meminta ma'af]
to arrive (vi)	datang	[dataŋ]
to ask (~ oneself)	bertanya	[bərtanja]
to ask (~ sb to do sth)	meminta	[meminta]
to be (~ a teacher)	ialah, adalah	[ialah], [adalah]
to be (~ on a diet)	sedang	[sedaŋ]
to be afraid	takut	[takut]
to be hungry	lapar	[lapar]
to be interested in ...	menaruh minat pada ...	[mənaruh minat pada ...]
to be needed	dibutuhkan	[dibutuhkan]
to be surprised	heran	[heran]
to be thirsty	haus	[haus]
to begin (vt)	memulai, membuka	[memulaj], [membuka]
to belong to ...	kepunyaan ...	[kepunja'an ...]
to boast (vi)	membual	[membual]
to break (split into pieces)	memecahkan	[memetʃahkan]
to call (~ for help)	memanggil	[memaŋgil]
can (v aux)	bisa	[bisa]
to catch (vt)	menangkap	[mənaŋkap]
to change (vt)	mengubah	[məŋubah]
to choose (select)	memilih	[memilih]
to come down (the stairs)	turun	[turun]
to compare (vt)	membandingkan	[membandiŋkan]
to complain (vi, vt)	mengeluh	[məŋeluh]
to confuse (mix up)	bingung membedakan	[biŋuŋ membedakan]
to continue (vt)	meneruskan	[mənəruskan]
to control (vt)	mengontrol	[məŋontrol]
to cook (dinner)	memasak	[memasa']
to cost (vt)	berharga	[bərharga]
to count (add up)	menghitung	[məŋhituŋ]
to count on ...	mengharapkan ...	[məŋharapkan ...]
to create (vt)	menciptakan	[məntʃiptakan]
to cry (weep)	menangis	[mənaŋis]

14. The most important verbs. Part 2

to deceive (vi, vt)	menipu	[mənipu]
to decorate (tree, street)	menghiasi	[məŋhiasi]
to defend (a country, etc.)	membela	[membela]
to demand (request firmly)	menuntut	[mənuntut]
to dig (vt)	menggali	[məŋgali]
to discuss (vt)	membicarakan	[membitʃarakan]
to do (vt)	membuat	[membuat]
to doubt (have doubts)	ragu-ragu	[ragu-ragu]
to drop (let fall)	tercecer	[tərtʃetʃer]
to enter (room, house, etc.)	masuk, memasuki	[masuk], [memasuki]
to excuse (forgive)	memaafkan	[memaʔafkan]
to exist (vi)	ada	[ada]
to expect (foresee)	menduga	[mənduga]
to explain (vt)	menjelaskan	[məndʒelaskan]
to fall (vi)	jatuh	[dʒʲatuh]
to find (vt)	menemukan	[mənemukan]
to finish (vt)	mengakhiri	[məŋahiri]
to fly (vi)	terbang	[tərbaŋ]
to follow … (come after)	mengikuti …	[məɲikuti …]
to forget (vi, vt)	melupakan	[melupakan]
to forgive (vt)	memaafkan	[memaʔafkan]
to give (vt)	memberi	[memberi]
to give a hint	memberi petunjuk	[memberi petundʒʲuʔ]
to go (on foot)	berjalan	[bərdʒʲalan]
to go for a swim	berenang	[bərenaŋ]
to go out (for dinner, etc.)	keluar	[keluar]
to guess (the answer)	menerka	[mənerka]
to have (vt)	mempunyai	[mempuɲaj]
to have breakfast	sarapan	[sarapan]
to have dinner	makan malam	[makan malam]
to have lunch	makan siang	[makan siaŋ]
to hear (vt)	mendengar	[məndeŋar]
to help (vt)	membantu	[membantu]
to hide (vt)	menyembunyikan	[məɲjembuɲikan]
to hope (vi, vt)	berharap	[bərharap]
to hunt (vi, vt)	berburu	[bərburu]
to hurry (vi)	tergesa-gesa	[tərgesa-gesa]

15. The most important verbs. Part 3

to inform (vt)	menginformasikan	[məɲinformasikan]
to insist (vi, vt)	mendesak	[məndesaʔ]
to insult (vt)	menghina	[məŋhina]
to invite (vt)	mengundang	[məŋundaŋ]
to joke (vi)	bergurau	[bərgurau]
to keep (vt)	menyimpan	[məɲimpan]
to keep silent	diam	[diam]
to kill (vt)	membunuh	[membunuh]
to know (sb)	kenal	[kenal]
to know (sth)	tahu	[tahu]
to laugh (vi)	tertawa	[tərtawa]
to liberate (city, etc.)	membebaskan	[membebaskan]
to like (I like …)	suka	[suka]
to look for … (search)	mencari …	[mənʧari …]
to love (sb)	mencintai	[mənʧintaj]
to make a mistake	salah	[salah]
to manage, to run	memimpin	[memimpin]
to mean (signify)	berarti	[berarti]
to mention (talk about)	menyebut	[mənjebut]
to miss (school, etc.)	absen	[absen]
to notice (see)	memperhatikan	[memperhatikan]
to object (vi, vt)	keberatan	[keberatan]
to observe (see)	mengamati	[məŋamati]
to open (vt)	membuka	[membuka]
to order (meal, etc.)	memesan	[memesan]
to order (mil.)	memerintahkan	[memerintahkan]
to own (possess)	memiliki	[memiliki]
to participate (vi)	turut serta	[turut serta]
to pay (vi, vt)	membayar	[membajar]
to permit (vt)	mengizinkan	[məɲizinkan]
to plan (vt)	merencanakan	[merenʧanakan]
to play (children)	bermain	[bərmajn]
to pray (vi, vt)	bersembahyang, berdoa	[bərsembahjaŋ], [bərdoa]
to prefer (vt)	lebih suka	[lebih suka]
to promise (vt)	berjanji	[bərdʒʲandʒi]
to pronounce (vt)	melafalkan	[melafalkan]
to propose (vt)	mengusulkan	[məŋusulkan]
to punish (vt)	menghukum	[məŋhukum]

16. The most important verbs. Part 4

| to read (vi, vt) | membaca | [membatʃa] |
| to recommend (vt) | merekomendasi | [merekomendasi] |

to refuse (vi, vt)	**menolak**	[mənolaʔ]
to regret (be sorry)	**menyesal**	[mənjesal]
to rent (sth from sb)	**menyewa**	[mənjewa]
to repeat (say again)	**mengulangi**	[məŋulaŋi]
to reserve, to book	**memesan**	[memesan]
to run (vi)	**lari**	[lari]
to save (rescue)	**menyelamatkan**	[mənjelamatkan]
to say (~ thank you)	**berkata**	[bərkata]
to scold (vt)	**memarahi, menegur**	[memarahi], [menegur]
to see (vt)	**melihat**	[melihat]
to sell (vt)	**menjual**	[məndʒˈual]
to send (vt)	**mengirim**	[məŋirim]
to shoot (vi)	**menembak**	[mənembaʔ]
to shout (vi)	**berteriak**	[bərteriaʔ]
to show (vt)	**menunjukkan**	[mənundʒˈuʔkan]
to sign (document)	**menandatangani**	[mənandataŋani]
to sit down (vi)	**duduk**	[duduʔ]
to smile (vi)	**tersenyum**	[tərsenyum]
to speak (vi, vt)	**berbicara**	[bərbitʃara]
to steal (money, etc.)	**mencuri**	[məntʃuri]
to stop (for pause, etc.)	**berhenti**	[bərhenti]
to stop (please ~ calling me)	**menghentikan**	[məŋhentikan]
to study (vt)	**mempelajari**	[mempeladʒˈari]
to swim (vi)	**berenang**	[bərenaŋ]
to take (vt)	**mengambil**	[məŋambil]
to think (vi, vt)	**berpikir**	[bərpikir]
to threaten (vt)	**mengancam**	[məŋantʃam]
to touch (with hands)	**menyentuh**	[mənjentuh]
to translate (vt)	**menerjemahkan**	[mənerdʒˈemahkan]
to trust (vt)	**mempercayai**	[mempertʃajaj]
to try (attempt)	**mencoba**	[məntʃoba]
to turn (e.g., ~ left)	**membelok**	[membeloʔ]
to underestimate (vt)	**meremehkan**	[meremehkan]
to understand (vt)	**mengerti**	[məŋerti]
to unite (vt)	**menyatukan**	[mənjatukan]
to wait (vt)	**menunggu**	[mənuŋgu]
to want (wish, desire)	**mau, ingin**	[mau], [iŋin]
to warn (vt)	**memperingatkan**	[memperiŋatkan]
to work (vi)	**bekerja**	[bekerdʒˈa]
to write (vt)	**menulis**	[mənulis]
to write down	**mencatat**	[məntʃatat]

TIME. CALENDAR

17. Weekdays

Monday	**Hari Senin**	[hari senin]
Tuesday	**Hari Selasa**	[hari selasa]
Wednesday	**Hari Rabu**	[hari rabu]
Thursday	**Hari Kamis**	[hari kamis]
Friday	**Hari Jumat**	[hari dʒʲumat]
Saturday	**Hari Sabtu**	[hari sabtu]
Sunday	**Hari Minggu**	[hari miŋgu]
today (adv)	**hari ini**	[hari ini]
tomorrow (adv)	**besok**	[besoˀ]
the day after tomorrow	**besok lusa**	[besoˀ lusa]
yesterday (adv)	**kemarin**	[kemarin]
the day before yesterday	**kemarin dulu**	[kemarin dulu]
day	**hari**	[hari]
working day	**hari kerja**	[hari kerdʒʲa]
public holiday	**hari libur**	[hari libur]
day off	**hari libur**	[hari libur]
weekend	**akhir pekan**	[ahir pekan]
all day long	**seharian**	[seharian]
the next day (adv)	**hari berikutnya**	[hari berikutnja]
two days ago	**dua hari lalu**	[dua hari lalu]
the day before	**hari sebelumnya**	[hari sebelumnja]
daily (adj)	**harian**	[harian]
every day (adv)	**tiap hari**	[tiap hari]
week	**minggu**	[miŋgu]
last week (adv)	**minggu lalu**	[miŋgu lalu]
next week (adv)	**minggu berikutnya**	[miŋgu berikutnja]
weekly (adj)	**mingguan**	[miŋguan]
every week (adv)	**tiap minggu**	[tiap miŋgu]
twice a week	**dua kali seminggu**	[dua kali semiŋgu]
every Tuesday	**tiap Hari Selasa**	[tiap hari selasa]

18. Hours. Day and night

morning	**pagi**	[pagi]
in the morning	**pada pagi hari**	[pada pagi hari]
noon, midday	**tengah hari**	[teŋah hari]

in the afternoon	**pada sore hari**	[pada sore hari]
evening	**sore, malam**	[sore], [malam]
in the evening	**waktu sore**	[waktu sore]
night	**malam**	[malam]
at night	**pada malam hari**	[pada malam hari]
midnight	**tengah malam**	[teŋah malam]
second	**detik**	[detiʔ]
minute	**menit**	[menit]
hour	**jam**	[dʒam]
half an hour	**setengah jam**	[seteŋah dʒam]
a quarter-hour	**seperempat jam**	[seperempat dʒam]
fifteen minutes	**lima belas menit**	[lima belas menit]
24 hours	**siang-malam**	[siaŋ-malam]
sunrise	**matahari terbit**	[matahari terbit]
dawn	**subuh**	[subuh]
early morning	**dini pagi**	[dini pagi]
sunset	**matahari terbenam**	[matahari terbenam]
early in the morning	**pagi-pagi**	[pagi-pagi]
this morning	**pagi ini**	[pagi ini]
tomorrow morning	**besok pagi**	[besoʔ pagi]
this afternoon	**sore ini**	[sore ini]
in the afternoon	**pada sore hari**	[pada sore hari]
tomorrow afternoon	**besok sore**	[besoʔ sore]
tonight (this evening)	**sore ini**	[sore ini]
tomorrow night	**besok malam**	[besoʔ malam]
at 3 o'clock sharp	**pukul 3 tepat**	[pukul tiga tepat]
about 4 o'clock	**sekitar pukul 4**	[sekitar pukul empat]
by 12 o'clock	**pada pukul 12**	[pada pukul belas]
in 20 minutes	**dalam 20 menit**	[dalam dua puluh menit]
in an hour	**dalam satu jam**	[dalam satu dʒam]
on time (adv)	**tepat waktu**	[tepat waktu]
a quarter of ...	**... kurang seperempat**	[... kuraŋ seperempat]
within an hour	**selama sejam**	[selama sedʒam]
every 15 minutes	**tiap 15 menit**	[tiap lima belas menit]
round the clock	**siang-malam**	[siaŋ-malam]

19. Months. Seasons

January	**Januari**	[dʒanuari]
February	**Februari**	[februari]
March	**Maret**	[maret]
April	**April**	[april]

May	**Mei**	[mei]
June	**Juni**	[dʒʲuni]
July	**Juli**	[dʒʲuli]
August	**Augustus**	[augustus]
September	**September**	[september]
October	**Oktober**	[oktober]
November	**November**	[november]
December	**Desember**	[desember]
spring	**musim semi**	[musim semi]
in spring	**pada musim semi**	[pada musim semi]
spring (as adj)	**musim semi**	[musim semi]
summer	**musim panas**	[musim panas]
in summer	**pada musim panas**	[pada musim panas]
summer (as adj)	**musim panas**	[musim panas]
fall	**musim gugur**	[musim gugur]
in fall	**pada musim gugur**	[pada musim gugur]
fall (as adj)	**musim gugur**	[musim gugur]
winter	**musim dingin**	[musim diŋin]
in winter	**pada musim dingin**	[pada musim diŋin]
winter (as adj)	**musim dingin**	[musim diŋin]
month	**bulan**	[bulan]
this month	**bulan ini**	[bulan ini]
next month	**bulan depan**	[bulan depan]
last month	**bulan lalu**	[bulan lalu]
a month ago	**sebulan lalu**	[sebulan lalu]
in a month (a month later)	**dalam satu bulan**	[dalam satu bulan]
in 2 months (2 months later)	**dalam 2 bulan**	[dalam dua bulan]
the whole month	**sepanjang bulan**	[sepandʒʲaŋ bulan]
all month long	**sebulan penuh**	[sebulan penuh]
monthly (~ magazine)	**bulanan**	[bulanan]
monthly (adv)	**tiap bulan**	[tiap bulan]
every month	**tiap bulan**	[tiap bulan]
twice a month	**dua kali sebulan**	[dua kali sebulan]
year	**tahun**	[tahun]
this year	**tahun ini**	[tahun ini]
next year	**tahun depan**	[tahun depan]
last year	**tahun lalu**	[tahun lalu]
a year ago	**setahun lalu**	[setahun lalu]
in a year	**dalam satu tahun**	[dalam satu tahun]
in two years	**dalam 2 tahun**	[dalam dua tahun]
the whole year	**sepanjang tahun**	[sepandʒʲaŋ tahun]

all year long	**setahun penuh**	[setahun penuh]
every year	**tiap tahun**	[tiap tahun]
annual (adj)	**tahunan**	[tahunan]
annually (adv)	**tiap tahun**	[tiap tahun]
4 times a year	**empat kali setahun**	[empat kali setahun]
date (e.g., today's ~)	**tanggal**	[taŋgal]
date (e.g., ~ of birth)	**tanggal**	[taŋgal]
calendar	**kalender**	[kalender]
half a year	**setengah tahun**	[seteŋah tahun]
six months	**enam bulan**	[enam bulan]
season (summer, etc.)	**musim**	[musim]
century	**abad**	[abad]

TRAVEL. HOTEL

20. Trip. Travel

tourism, travel	**pariwisata**	[pariwisata]
tourist	**turis, wisatawan**	[turis], [wisatawan]
trip, voyage	**pengembaraan**	[peɲembara'an]
adventure	**petualangan**	[petualaŋan]
trip, journey	**perjalanan, lawatan**	[perdʒ'alanan], [lawatan]
vacation	**liburan**	[liburan]
to be on vacation	**berlibur**	[bərlibur]
rest	**istirahat**	[istirahat]
train	**kereta api**	[kereta api]
by train	**naik kereta api**	[nai' kereta api]
airplane	**pesawat terbang**	[pesawat tərbaŋ]
by airplane	**naik pesawat terbang**	[nai' pesawat tərbaŋ]
by car	**naik mobil**	[nai' mobil]
by ship	**naik kapal**	[nai' kapal]
luggage	**bagasi**	[bagasi]
suitcase	**koper**	[koper]
luggage cart	**troli bagasi**	[troli bagasi]
passport	**paspor**	[paspor]
visa	**visa**	[visa]
ticket	**tiket**	[tiket]
air ticket	**tiket pesawat terbang**	[tiket pesawat tərbaŋ]
guidebook	**buku pedoman**	[buku pedoman]
map (tourist ~)	**peta**	[peta]
area (rural ~)	**kawasan**	[kawasan]
place, site	**tempat**	[tempat]
exotica (n)	**keeksotisan**	[keeksotisan]
exotic (adj)	**eksotis**	[eksotis]
amazing (adj)	**menakjubkan**	[mənakdʒ'ubkan]
group	**kelompok**	[kelompo']
excursion, sightseeing tour	**ekskursi**	[ekskursi]
guide (person)	**pemandu wisata**	[pemandu wisata]

21. Hotel

hotel, inn	**hotel**	[hotel]
motel	**motel**	[motel]
three-star (~ hotel)	**bintang tiga**	[bintaŋ tiga]
five-star	**bintang lima**	[bintaŋ lima]
to stay (in a hotel, etc.)	**menginap**	[məŋinap]
room	**kamar**	[kamar]
single room	**kamar tunggal**	[kamar tuŋgal]
double room	**kamar ganda**	[kamar ganda]
to book a room	**memesan kamar**	[memesan kamar]
half board	**sewa setengah**	[sewa seteŋah]
full board	**sewa penuh**	[sewa penuh]
with bath	**dengan kamar mandi**	[deŋan kamar mandi]
with shower	**dengan pancuran**	[deŋan pantʃuran]
satellite television	**televisi satelit**	[televisi satelit]
air-conditioner	**penyejuk udara**	[penjedʒｊuʔ udara]
towel	**handuk**	[handuʔ]
key	**kunci**	[kuntʃi]
administrator	**administrator**	[administrator]
chambermaid	**pelayan kamar**	[pelajan kamar]
porter, bellboy	**porter**	[porter]
doorman	**pramupintu**	[pramupintu]
restaurant	**restoran**	[restoran]
pub, bar	**bar**	[bar]
breakfast	**makan pagi, sarapan**	[makan pagi], [sarapan]
dinner	**makan malam**	[makan malam]
buffet	**prasmanan**	[prasmanan]
lobby	**lobi**	[lobi]
elevator	**elevator**	[elevator]
DO NOT DISTURB	**JANGAN MENGGANGGU**	[dʒｊaŋan meŋgaŋgu]
NO SMOKING	**DILARANG MEROKOK!**	[dilaraŋ merokoʔ!]

22. Sightseeing

monument	**monumen, patung**	[monumen], [patuŋ]
fortress	**benteng**	[benteŋ]
palace	**istana**	[istana]
castle	**kastil**	[kastil]
tower	**menara**	[mənara]

mausoleum	**mausoleum**	[mausoleum]
architecture	**arsitektur**	[arsitektur]
medieval (adj)	**abad pertengahan**	[abad perteŋahan]
ancient (adj)	**kuno**	[kuno]
national (adj)	**nasional**	[nasional]
famous (monument, etc.)	**terkenal**	[terkenal]
tourist	**turis, wisatawan**	[turis], [wisatawan]
guide (person)	**pemandu wisata**	[pemandu wisata]
excursion, sightseeing tour	**ekskursi**	[ekskursi]
to show (vt)	**menunjukkan**	[menundʒiuʔkan]
to tell (vt)	**menceritakan**	[mentʃeritakan]
to find (vt)	**mendapatkan**	[mendapatkan]
to get lost (lose one's way)	**tersesat**	[tersesat]
map (e.g., subway ~)	**denah**	[denah]
map (e.g., city ~)	**peta**	[peta]
souvenir, gift	**suvenir**	[suvenir]
gift shop	**toko suvenir**	[toko suvenir]
to take pictures	**memotret**	[memotret]
to have one's picture taken	**berfoto**	[berfoto]

TRANSPORTATION

23. Airport

airport	**bandara**	[bandara]
airplane	**pesawat terbang**	[pesawat tərbaŋ]
airline	**maskapai penerbangan**	[maskapaj penerbaŋan]
air traffic controller	**pengawas lalu lintas udara**	[peŋawas lalu lintas udara]
departure	**keberangkatan**	[keberaŋkatan]
arrival	**kedatangan**	[kedataŋan]
to arrive (by plane)	**datang**	[dataŋ]
departure time	**waktu keberangkatan**	[waktu keberaŋkatan]
arrival time	**waktu kedatangan**	[waktu kedataŋan]
to be delayed	**terlambat**	[tərlambat]
flight delay	**penundaan penerbangan**	[penunda'an penerbaŋan]
information board	**papan informasi**	[papan informasi]
information	**informasi**	[informasi]
to announce (vt)	**mengumumkan**	[meŋumumkan]
flight (e.g., next ~)	**penerbangan**	[penerbaŋan]
customs	**pabean**	[pabean]
customs officer	**petugas pabean**	[petugas pabean]
customs declaration	**pernyataan pabean**	[pərnjata'an pabean]
to fill out (vt)	**mengisi**	[meŋisi]
to fill out the declaration	**mengisi formulir bea cukai**	[meŋisi formulir bea tʃukaj]
passport control	**pemeriksaan paspor**	[pemeriksa'an paspor]
luggage	**bagasi**	[bagasi]
hand luggage	**jinjingan**	[dʒindʒiŋan]
luggage cart	**troli bagasi**	[troli bagasi]
landing	**pendaratan**	[pendaratan]
landing strip	**jalur pendaratan**	[dʒ'alur pendaratan]
to land (vi)	**mendarat**	[mendarat]
airstairs	**tangga pesawat**	[taŋga pesawat]
check-in	**check-in**	[tʃekin]
check-in counter	**meja check-in**	[medʒ'a tʃekin]
to check-in (vi)	**check-in**	[tʃekin]

boarding pass	kartu pas	[kartu pas]
departure gate	gerbang keberangkatan	[gerbaŋ keberaŋkatan]
transit	transit	[transit]
to wait (vt)	menunggu	[mənuŋgu]
departure lounge	ruang tunggu	[ruaŋ tuŋgu]
to see off	mengantar	[məŋantar]
to say goodbye	berpamitan	[bərpamitan]

24. Airplane

airplane	pesawat terbang	[pesawat tərbaŋ]
air ticket	tiket pesawat terbang	[tiket pesawat tərbaŋ]
airline	maskapai penerbangan	[maskapaj penerbaŋan]
airport	bandara	[bandara]
supersonic (adj)	supersonik	[supersoniʔ]
captain	kapten	[kapten]
crew	awak	[awaʔ]
pilot	pilot	[pilot]
flight attendant (fem.)	pramugari	[pramugari]
navigator	navigator, penavigasi	[navigator], [penavigasi]
wings	sayap	[sajap]
tail	ekor	[ekor]
cockpit	kokpit	[kokpit]
engine	mesin	[mesin]
undercarriage (landing gear)	roda pendarat	[roda pendarat]
turbine	turbin	[turbin]
propeller	baling-baling	[baliŋ-baliŋ]
black box	kotak hitam	[kotaʔ hitam]
yoke (control column)	kemudi	[kemudi]
fuel	bahan bakar	[bahan bakar]
safety card	instruksi keselamatan	[instruksi keselamatan]
oxygen mask	masker oksigen	[masker oksigen]
uniform	seragam	[seragam]
life vest	jaket pelampung	[dʒʲaket pelampuŋ]
parachute	parasut	[parasut]
takeoff	lepas landas	[lepas landas]
to take off (vi)	bertolak	[bertolaʔ]
runway	jalur lepas landas	[dʒʲalur lepas landas]
visibility	visibilitas, pandangan	[visibilitas], [pandaŋan]
flight (act of flying)	penerbangan	[penerbaŋan]
altitude	ketinggian	[ketiŋgian]
air pocket	lubang udara	[lubaŋ udara]

seat	**tempat duduk**	[tempat dudu?]
headphones	**headphone, fonkepala**	[headphone], [fonkepala]
folding tray (tray table)	**meja lipat**	[medʒʲa lipat]
airplane window	**jendela pesawat**	[dʒʲendela pesawat]
aisle	**lorong**	[loroŋ]

25. Train

train	**kereta api**	[kereta api]
commuter train	**kereta api listrik**	[kereta api listri?]
express train	**kereta api cepat**	[kereta api tʃepat]
diesel locomotive	**lokomotif diesel**	[lokomotif disel]
steam locomotive	**lokomotif uap**	[lokomotif uap]
passenger car	**gerbong penumpang**	[gerboŋ penumpaŋ]
dining car	**gerbong makan**	[gerboŋ makan]
rails	**rel**	[rel]
railroad	**rel kereta api**	[rel kereta api]
railway tie	**bantalan rel**	[bantalan rel]
platform (railway ~)	**platform**	[platform]
track (~ 1, 2, etc.)	**jalur**	[dʒʲalur]
semaphore	**semafor**	[semafor]
station	**stasiun**	[stasiun]
engineer (train driver)	**masinis**	[masinis]
porter (of luggage)	**porter**	[porter]
car attendant	**kondektur**	[kondektur]
passenger	**penumpang**	[penumpaŋ]
conductor (ticket inspector)	**kondektur**	[kondektur]
corridor (in train)	**koridor**	[koridor]
emergency brake	**rem darurat**	[rem darurat]
compartment	**kabin**	[kabin]
berth	**bangku**	[baŋku]
upper berth	**bangku atas**	[baŋku atas]
lower berth	**bangku bawah**	[baŋku bawah]
bed linen, bedding	**kain kasur**	[kain kasur]
ticket	**tiket**	[tiket]
schedule	**jadwal**	[dʒʲadwal]
information display	**layar informasi**	[lajar informasi]
to leave, to depart	**berangkat**	[beraŋkat]
departure (of train)	**keberangkatan**	[keberaŋkatan]
to arrive (ab. train)	**datang**	[dataŋ]
arrival	**kedatangan**	[kedataŋan]

to arrive by train	datang naik kereta api	[dataŋ naj' kereta api]
to get on the train	naik ke kereta	[nai' ke kereta]
to get off the train	turun dari kereta	[turun dari kereta]
train wreck	kecelakaan kereta	[ketʃelaka'an kereta]
to derail (vi)	keluar rel	[keluar rel]
steam locomotive	lokomotif uap	[lokomotif uap]
stoker, fireman	juru api	[dʒ'uru api]
firebox	tungku	[tuŋku]
coal	batu bara	[batu bara]

26. Ship

ship	kapal	[kapal]
vessel	kapal	[kapal]
steamship	kapal uap	[kapal uap]
riverboat	kapal api	[kapal api]
cruise ship	kapal laut	[kapal laut]
cruiser	kapal penjelajah	[kapal pendʒ'eladʒ'ah]
yacht	perahu pesiar	[pərahu pesiar]
tugboat	kapal tunda	[kapal tunda]
barge	tongkang	[toŋkaŋ]
ferry	feri	[feri]
sailing ship	kapal layar	[kapal lajar]
brigantine	kapal brigantin	[kapal brigantin]
ice breaker	kapal pemecah es	[kapal pemetʃah es]
submarine	kapal selam	[kapal selam]
boat (flat-bottomed ~)	perahu	[pərahu]
dinghy	sekoci	[sekotʃi]
lifeboat	sekoci penyelamat	[sekotʃi penjelamat]
motorboat	perahu motor	[pərahu motor]
captain	kapten	[kapten]
seaman	kelasi	[kelasi]
sailor	pelaut	[pelaut]
crew	awak	[awa']
boatswain	bosman, bosun	[bosman], [bosun]
ship's boy	kadet laut	[kadet laut]
cook	koki	[koki]
ship's doctor	dokter kapal	[dokter kapal]
deck	dek	[de']
mast	tiang	[tiaŋ]

sail	**layar**	[lajar]
hold	**lambung kapal**	[lambuŋ kapal]
bow (prow)	**haluan**	[haluan]
stern	**buritan**	[buritan]
oar	**dayung**	[dajuŋ]
screw propeller	**baling-baling**	[baliŋ-baliŋ]

cabin	**kabin**	[kabin]
wardroom	**ruang rekreasi**	[ruaŋ rekreasi]
engine room	**ruang mesin**	[ruaŋ mesin]
bridge	**anjungan kapal**	[andʒˈuŋan kapal]
radio room	**ruang radio**	[ruaŋ radio]
wave (radio)	**gelombang radio**	[gelombaŋ radio]
logbook	**buku harian kapal**	[buku harian kapal]

spyglass	**teropong**	[təropoŋ]
bell	**lonceng**	[lontʃeŋ]
flag	**bendera**	[bendera]

| hawser (mooring ~) | **tali** | [tali] |
| knot (bowline, etc.) | **simpul** | [simpul] |

| deckrails | **pegangan** | [pegaŋan] |
| gangway | **tangga kapal** | [taŋga kapal] |

anchor	**jangkar**	[dʒˈaŋkar]
to weigh anchor	**mengangkat jangkar**	[məŋaŋkat dʒˈaŋkar]
to drop anchor	**menjatuhkan jangkar**	[məndʒˈatuhkan dʒˈaŋkar]
anchor chain	**rantai jangkar**	[rantaj dʒˈaŋkar]

port (harbor)	**pelabuhan**	[pelabuhan]
quay, wharf	**dermaga**	[dermaga]
to berth (moor)	**merapat**	[merapat]
to cast off	**bertolak**	[bərtolaʔ]

trip, voyage	**pengembaraan**	[peŋembara'an]
cruise (sea trip)	**pesiar**	[pesiar]
course (route)	**haluan**	[haluan]
route (itinerary)	**rute**	[rute]

| shallows | **beting** | [betiŋ] |
| to run aground | **kandas** | [kandas] |

storm	**badai**	[badaj]
signal	**sinyal**	[sinjal]
to sink (vi)	**tenggelam**	[teŋgelam]
Man overboard!	**Orang hanyut!**	[oraŋ hanyut!]
SOS (distress signal)	**SOS**	[es-o-es]
ring buoy	**pelampung penyelamat**	[pelampuŋ penjelamat]

CITY

27. Urban transportation

bus	**bus**	[bus]
streetcar	**trem**	[trem]
trolley bus	**bus listrik**	[bus listriʔ]
route (of bus, etc.)	**trayek**	[traeʔ]
number (e.g., bus ~)	**nomor**	[nomor]
to go by ...	**naik ...**	[naiʔ ...]
to get on (~ the bus)	**naik**	[naiʔ]
to get off ...	**turun ...**	[turun ...]
stop (e.g., bus ~)	**halte, pemberhentian**	[halte], [pemberhentian]
next stop	**halte berikutnya**	[halte berikutnja]
terminus	**halte terakhir**	[halte terahir]
schedule	**jadwal**	[dʒʲadwal]
to wait (vt)	**menunggu**	[menuŋgu]
ticket	**tiket**	[tiket]
fare	**harga karcis**	[harga kartʃis]
cashier (ticket seller)	**kasir**	[kasir]
ticket inspection	**pemeriksaan tiket**	[pemeriksaʔan tiket]
ticket inspector	**kondektur**	[kondektur]
to be late (for ...)	**terlambat ...**	[terlambat ...]
to miss (~ the train, etc.)	**ketinggalan**	[ketiŋgalan]
to be in a hurry	**tergesa-gesa**	[tergesa-gesa]
taxi, cab	**taksi**	[taksi]
taxi driver	**sopir taksi**	[sopir taksi]
by taxi	**naik taksi**	[naiʔ taksi]
taxi stand	**pangkalan taksi**	[paŋkalan taksi]
to call a taxi	**memanggil taksi**	[memaŋgil taksi]
to take a taxi	**menaiki taksi**	[menajki taksi]
traffic	**lalu lintas**	[lalu lintas]
traffic jam	**kemacetan lalu lintas**	[kematʃetan lalu lintas]
rush hour	**jam sibuk**	[dʒʲam sibuʔ]
to park (vi)	**parkir**	[parkir]
to park (vt)	**memarkir**	[memarkir]
parking lot	**tempat parkir**	[tempat parkir]
subway	**kereta api bawah tanah**	[kereta api bawah tanah]
station	**stasiun**	[stasiun]

to take the subway	naik kereta api bawah tanah	[nai' kereta api bawah tanah]
train	kereta api	[kereta api]
train station	stasiun kereta api	[stasiun kereta api]

28. City. Life in the city

city, town	kota	[kota]
capital city	ibu kota	[ibu kota]
village	desa	[desa]

city map	peta kota	[peta kota]
downtown	pusat kota	[pusat kota]
suburb	pinggir kota	[piŋgir kota]
suburban (adj)	pinggir kota	[piŋgir kota]

outskirts	pinggir	[piŋgir]
environs (suburbs)	daerah sekitarnya	[daerah sekitarnja]
city block	blok	[blo']
residential block (area)	blok perumahan	[blo' perumahan]

traffic	lalu lintas	[lalu lintas]
traffic lights	lampu lalu lintas	[lampu lalu lintas]
public transportation	angkot	[aŋkot]
intersection	persimpangan	[persimpaŋan]

crosswalk	penyeberangan	[penjeberaŋan]
pedestrian underpass	terowongan penyeberangan	[terowoŋan penjeberaŋan]
to cross (~ the street)	menyeberang	[menjeberaŋ]
pedestrian	pejalan kaki	[pedʒʲalan kaki]
sidewalk	trotoar	[trotoar]

bridge	jembatan	[dʒʲembatan]
embankment (river walk)	tepi sungai	[tepi suŋaj]
fountain	air mancur	[air mantʃur]

allée (garden walkway)	jalan kecil	[dʒʲalan ketʃil]
park	taman	[taman]
boulevard	bulevar, adimarga	[bulevar], [adimarga]
square	lapangan	[lapaŋan]
avenue (wide street)	jalan raya	[dʒʲalan raja]
street	jalan	[dʒʲalan]
side street	gang	[gaŋ]
dead end	jalan buntu	[dʒʲalan buntu]

house	rumah	[rumah]
building	gedung	[geduŋ]
skyscraper	pencakar langit	[pentʃakar laŋit]
facade	bagian depan	[bagian depan]

roof	**atap**	[atap]
window	**jendela**	[dʒʲendela]
arch	**lengkungan**	[leŋkuŋan]
column	**pilar**	[pilar]
corner	**sudut**	[sudut]

store window	**etalase**	[etalase]
signboard (store sign, etc.)	**papan nama**	[papan nama]
poster	**poster**	[poster]
advertising poster	**poster iklan**	[poster iklan]
billboard	**papan iklan**	[papan iklan]

garbage, trash	**sampah**	[sampah]
trashcan (public ~)	**tong sampah**	[toŋ sampah]
to litter (vi)	**menyampah**	[mənjampah]
garbage dump	**tempat pemrosesan akhir (TPA)**	[tempat pemrosesan ahir]

phone booth	**gardu telepon umum**	[gardu telepon umum]
lamppost	**tiang lampu**	[tiaŋ lampu]
bench (park ~)	**bangku**	[baŋku]

police officer	**polisi**	[polisi]
police	**polisi, kepolisian**	[polisi], [kepolisian]
beggar	**pengemis**	[peɲemis]
homeless (n)	**tuna wisma**	[tuna wisma]

29. Urban institutions

store	**toko**	[toko]
drugstore, pharmacy	**apotek, toko obat**	[apotek], [toko obat]
eyeglass store	**optik**	[optiʔ]
shopping mall	**toserba**	[toserba]
supermarket	**pasar swalayan**	[pasar swalajan]

bakery	**toko roti**	[toko roti]
baker	**pembuat roti**	[pembuat roti]
pastry shop	**toko kue**	[toko kue]
grocery store	**toko pangan**	[toko paɲan]
butcher shop	**toko daging**	[toko dagiɲ]

| produce store | **toko sayur** | [toko sajur] |
| market | **pasar** | [pasar] |

coffee house	**warung kopi**	[waruŋ kopi]
restaurant	**restoran**	[restoran]
pub, bar	**kedai bir**	[kedaj bir]
pizzeria	**kedai piza**	[kedaj piza]
hair salon	**salon rambut**	[salon rambut]
post office	**kantor pos**	[kantor pos]

dry cleaners	**penatu kimia**	[penatu kimia]
photo studio	**studio foto**	[studio foto]
shoe store	**toko sepatu**	[toko sepatu]
bookstore	**toko buku**	[toko buku]
sporting goods store	**toko alat olahraga**	[toko alat olahraga]
clothes repair shop	**reparasi pakaian**	[reparasi pakajan]
formal wear rental	**rental pakaian**	[rental pakajan]
video rental store	**rental film**	[rental film]
circus	**sirkus**	[sirkus]
zoo	**kebun binatang**	[kebun binataŋ]
movie theater	**bioskop**	[bioskop]
museum	**museum**	[museum]
library	**perpustakaan**	[pərpustakaʔan]
theater	**teater**	[teater]
opera (opera house)	**opera**	[opera]
nightclub	**klub malam**	[klub malam]
casino	**kasino**	[kasino]
mosque	**masjid**	[masdʒid]
synagogue	**sinagoga, kanisah**	[sinagoga], [kanisah]
cathedral	**katedral**	[katedral]
temple	**kuil, candi**	[kuil], [tʃandi]
church	**gereja**	[geredʒʲa]
college	**institut, perguruan tinggi**	[institut], [pərguruan tiŋgi]
university	**universitas**	[universitas]
school	**sekolah**	[sekolah]
prefecture	**prefektur, distrik**	[prefektur], [distriʔ]
city hall	**balai kota**	[balaj kota]
hotel	**hotel**	[hotel]
bank	**bank**	[banʔ]
embassy	**kedutaan besar**	[kedutaʔan besar]
travel agency	**kantor pariwisata**	[kantor pariwisata]
information office	**kantor penerangan**	[kantor peneraŋan]
currency exchange	**kantor penukaran uang**	[kantor penukaran uaŋ]
subway	**kereta api bawah tanah**	[kereta api bawah tanah]
hospital	**rumah sakit**	[rumah sakit]
gas station	**SPBU,** **stasiun bensin**	[es-pe-be-u], [stasjun bensin]
parking lot	**tempat parkir**	[tempat parkir]

30. Signs

signboard (store sign, etc.)	**papan nama**	[papan nama]
notice (door sign, etc.)	**tulisan**	[tulisan]
poster	**poster**	[poster]
direction sign	**penunjuk arah**	[penundʒiuˀ arah]
arrow (sign)	**anak panah**	[anaˀ panah]
caution	**peringatan**	[periŋatan]
warning sign	**tanda peringatan**	[tanda periŋatan]
to warn (vt)	**memperingatkan**	[memperiŋatkan]
rest day (weekly ~)	**hari libur**	[hari libur]
timetable (schedule)	**jadwal**	[dʒiadwal]
opening hours	**jam buka**	[dʒiam buka]
WELCOME!	**SELAMAT DATANG!**	[selamat dataŋ!]
ENTRANCE	**MASUK**	[masuˀ]
EXIT	**KELUAR**	[keluar]
PUSH	**DORONG**	[doroŋ]
PULL	**TARIK**	[tariˀ]
OPEN	**BUKA**	[buka]
CLOSED	**TUTUP**	[tutup]
WOMEN	**WANITA**	[wanita]
MEN	**PRIA**	[pria]
DISCOUNTS	**DISKON**	[diskon]
SALE	**OBRAL**	[obral]
NEW!	**BARU!**	[baru!]
FREE	**GRATIS**	[gratis]
ATTENTION!	**PERHATIAN!**	[perhatian!]
NO VACANCIES	**PENUH**	[penuh]
RESERVED	**DIRESERVASI**	[direservasi]
ADMINISTRATION	**ADMINISTRASI**	[administrasi]
STAFF ONLY	**KHUSUS STAF**	[husus staf]
BEWARE OF THE DOG!	**AWAS, ANJING GALAK!**	[awas], [andʒiŋ galaˀ!]
NO SMOKING	**DILARANG MEROKOK!**	[dilaraŋ merokoˀ!]
DO NOT TOUCH!	**JANGAN SENTUH!**	[dʒiaŋan sentuh!]
DANGEROUS	**BERBAHAYA**	[berbahaja]
DANGER	**BAHAYA**	[bahaja]
HIGH VOLTAGE	**TEGANGAN TINGGI**	[tegaŋan tiŋgi]
NO SWIMMING!	**DILARANG BERENANG!**	[dilaraŋ berenaŋ!]
OUT OF ORDER	**RUSAK**	[rusaˀ]
FLAMMABLE	**BAHAN MUDAH TERBAKAR**	[bahan mudah terbakar]

FORBIDDEN	**DILARANG**	[dilaraŋ]
NO TRESPASSING!	**DILARANG MASUK!**	[dilaraŋ masuʔl]
WET PAINT	**AWAS CAT BASAH**	[awas tʃat basah]

31. Shopping

to buy (purchase)	**membeli**	[membeli]
purchase	**belanjaan**	[belandʒiaʼan]
to go shopping	**berbelanja**	[bərbelandʒia]
shopping	**berbelanja**	[bərbelandʒia]

| to be open (ab. store) | **buka** | [buka] |
| to be closed | **tutup** | [tutup] |

footwear, shoes	**sepatu**	[sepatu]
clothes, clothing	**pakaian**	[pakajan]
cosmetics	**kosmetik**	[kosmetiʔ]
food products	**produk makanan**	[produʼ makanan]
gift, present	**hadiah**	[hadiah]

| salesman | **pramuniaga** | [pramuniaga] |
| saleswoman | **pramuniaga perempuan** | [pramuniaga pərempuan] |

check out, cash desk	**kas**	[kas]
mirror	**cermin**	[tʃermin]
counter (store ~)	**konter**	[konter]
fitting room	**kamar pas**	[kamar pas]

to try on	**mengepas**	[məŋepas]
to fit (ab. dress, etc.)	**pas, cocok**	[pas], [tʃotʃoʼ]
to like (I like ...)	**suka**	[suka]

price	**harga**	[harga]
price tag	**label harga**	[label harga]
to cost (vt)	**berharga**	[bərharga]
How much?	**Berapa?**	[bərapa?]
discount	**diskon**	[diskon]

inexpensive (adj)	**tidak mahal**	[tidaʼ mahal]
cheap (adj)	**murah**	[murah]
expensive (adj)	**mahal**	[mahal]
It's expensive	**Ini mahal**	[ini mahal]

rental (n)	**rental, persewaan**	[rental], [pərsewaʼan]
to rent (~ a tuxedo)	**menyewa**	[mənjewa]
credit (trade credit)	**kredit**	[kredit]
on credit (adv)	**secara kredit**	[setʃara kredit]

CLOTHING & ACCESSORIES

32. Outerwear. Coats

clothes	pakaian	[pakajan]
outerwear	pakaian luar	[pakajan luar]
winter clothing	pakaian musim dingin	[pakajan musim diŋin]
coat (overcoat)	mantel	[mantel]
fur coat	mantel bulu	[mantel bulu]
fur jacket	jaket bulu	[dʒʲaket bulu]
down coat	jaket bulu halus	[dʒʲaket bulu halus]
jacket (e.g., leather ~)	jaket	[dʒʲaket]
raincoat (trenchcoat, etc.)	jas hujan	[dʒʲas hudʒʲan]
waterproof (adj)	kedap air	[kedap air]

33. Men's & women's clothing

shirt (button shirt)	kemeja	[kemedʒʲa]
pants	celana	[tʃelana]
jeans	celana jins	[tʃelana dʒins]
suit jacket	jas	[dʒʲas]
suit	setelan	[setelan]
dress (frock)	gaun	[gaun]
skirt	rok	[roʔ]
blouse	blus	[blus]
knitted jacket (cardigan, etc.)	jaket wol	[dʒʲaket wol]
jacket (of woman's suit)	jaket	[dʒʲaket]
T-shirt	baju kaus	[badʒʲu kaus]
shorts (short trousers)	celana pendek	[tʃelana pendeʔ]
tracksuit	pakaian olahraga	[pakajan olahraga]
bathrobe	jubah mandi	[dʒʲubah mandi]
pajamas	piyama	[piyama]
sweater	sweter	[sweter]
pullover	pulover	[pulover]
vest	rompi	[rompi]
tailcoat	jas berbuntut	[dʒʲas berbuntut]
tuxedo	jas malam	[dʒʲas malam]

uniform	**seragam**	[seragam]
workwear	**pakaian kerja**	[pakajan kerdʒʲa]
overalls	**baju monyet**	[badʒʲu monjet]
coat (e.g., doctor's smock)	**jas**	[dʒʲas]

34. Clothing. Underwear

underwear	**pakaian dalam**	[pakajan dalam]
boxers, briefs	**celana dalam lelaki**	[tʃelana dalam lelaki]
panties	**celana dalam wanita**	[tʃelana dalam wanita]
undershirt (A-shirt)	**singlet**	[siŋlet]
socks	**kaus kaki**	[kaus kaki]

nightgown	**baju tidur**	[badʒʲu tidur]
bra	**beha**	[beha]
knee highs (knee-high socks)	**kaus kaki selutut**	[kaus kaki selutut]
pantyhose	**pantihos**	[pantihos]
stockings (thigh highs)	**kaus kaki panjang**	[kaus kaki pandʒʲaŋ]
bathing suit	**baju renang**	[badʒʲu renaŋ]

35. Headwear

hat	**topi**	[topi]
fedora	**topi bulat**	[topi bulat]
baseball cap	**topi bisbol**	[topi bisbol]
flatcap	**topi pet**	[topi pet]

beret	**baret**	[baret]
hood	**kerudung kepala**	[keruduŋ kepala]
panama hat	**topi panama**	[topi panama]
knit cap (knitted hat)	**topi rajut**	[topi radʒʲut]

headscarf	**tudung kepala**	[tuduŋ kepala]
women's hat	**topi wanita**	[topi wanita]
hard hat	**topi baja**	[topi badʒʲa]
garrison cap	**topi lipat**	[topi lipat]
helmet	**helm**	[helm]

| derby | **topi bulat** | [topi bulat] |
| top hat | **topi tinggi** | [topi tiŋgi] |

36. Footwear

| footwear | **sepatu** | [sepatu] |
| shoes (men's shoes) | **sepatu bot** | [sepatu bot] |

shoes (women's shoes)	**sepatu wanita**	[sepatu wanita]
boots (e.g., cowboy ~)	**sepatu lars**	[sepatu lars]
slippers	**pantofel**	[pantofel]
tennis shoes (e.g., Nike ~)	**sepatu tenis**	[sepatu tenis]
sneakers	**sepatu kets**	[sepatu kets]
(e.g., Converse ~)		
sandals	**sandal**	[sandal]
cobbler (shoe repairer)	**tukang sepatu**	[tukaŋ sepatu]
heel	**tumit**	[tumit]
pair (of shoes)	**sepasang**	[sepasaŋ]
shoestring	**tali sepatu**	[tali sepatu]
to lace (vt)	**mengikat tali**	[məŋikat tali]
shoehorn	**sendok sepatu**	[sendo' sepatu]
shoe polish	**semir sepatu**	[semir sepatu]

37. Personal accessories

gloves	**sarung tangan**	[saruŋ taŋan]
mittens	**sarung tangan**	[saruŋ taŋan]
scarf (muffler)	**selendang**	[selendaŋ]
glasses (eyeglasses)	**kacamata**	[katʃamata]
frame (eyeglass ~)	**bingkai**	[biŋkaj]
umbrella	**payung**	[pajuŋ]
walking stick	**tongkat jalan**	[toŋkat dʒʲalan]
hairbrush	**sikat rambut**	[sikat rambut]
fan	**kipas**	[kipas]
tie (necktie)	**dasi**	[dasi]
bow tie	**dasi kupu-kupu**	[dasi kupu-kupu]
suspenders	**bretel**	[bretel]
handkerchief	**sapu tangan**	[sapu taŋan]
comb	**sisir**	[sisir]
barrette	**jepit rambut**	[dʒʲepit rambut]
hairpin	**harnal**	[harnal]
buckle	**gesper**	[gesper]
belt	**sabuk**	[sabu']
shoulder strap	**tali tas**	[tali tas]
bag (handbag)	**tas**	[tas]
purse	**tas tangan**	[tas taŋan]
backpack	**ransel**	[ransel]

38. Clothing. Miscellaneous

fashion	**mode**	[mode]
in vogue (adj)	**modis**	[modis]
fashion designer	**perancang busana**	[perantʃaŋ busana]
collar	**kerah**	[kerah]
pocket	**saku**	[saku]
pocket (as adj)	**saku**	[saku]
sleeve	**lengan**	[leŋan]
hanging loop	**tali kait**	[tali kait]
fly (on trousers)	**golbi**	[golbi]
zipper (fastener)	**ritsleting**	[ritsletiŋ]
fastener	**kancing**	[kantʃiŋ]
button	**kancing**	[kantʃiŋ]
buttonhole	**lubang kancing**	[lubaŋ kantʃiŋ]
to come off (ab. button)	**terlepas**	[tərlepas]
to sew (vi, vt)	**menjahit**	[məndʒʲahit]
to embroider (vi, vt)	**membordir**	[membordir]
embroidery	**bordiran**	[bordiran]
sewing needle	**jarum**	[dʒʲarum]
thread	**benang**	[benaŋ]
seam	**setik**	[setiʔ]
to get dirty (vi)	**kena kotor**	[kena kotor]
stain (mark, spot)	**bercak**	[bertʃaʔ]
to crease, crumple (vi)	**kumal**	[kumal]
to tear, to rip (vt)	**merobek**	[merobeʔ]
clothes moth	**ngengat**	[ŋeŋat]

39. Personal care. Cosmetics

toothpaste	**pasta gigi**	[pasta gigi]
toothbrush	**sikat gigi**	[sikat gigi]
to brush one's teeth	**menggosok gigi**	[məŋgoso' gigi]
razor	**pisau cukur**	[pisau tʃukur]
shaving cream	**krim cukur**	[krim tʃukur]
to shave (vi)	**bercukur**	[bərtʃukur]
soap	**sabun**	[sabun]
shampoo	**sampo**	[sampo]
scissors	**gunting**	[guntiŋ]
nail file	**kikir kuku**	[kikir kuku]
nail clippers	**pemotong kuku**	[pemotoŋ kuku]
tweezers	**pinset**	[pinset]

cosmetics	kosmetik	[kosmeti']
face mask	masker	[masker]
manicure	manikur	[manikur]
to have a manicure	melakukan manikur	[melakukan manikur]
pedicure	pedi	[pedi]

make-up bag	tas kosmetik	[tas kosmeti']
face powder	bedak	[beda']
powder compact	kotak bedak	[kota' beda']
blusher	perona pipi	[perona pipi]

perfume (bottled)	parfum	[parfum]
toilet water (lotion)	minyak wangi	[minja' waŋi]
lotion	losion	[losjon]
cologne	kolonye	[kolone]

eyeshadow	pewarna mata	[pewarna mata]
eyeliner	pensil alis	[pensil alis]
mascara	celak	[tʃela']

lipstick	lipstik	[lipsti']
nail polish, enamel	kuteks, cat kuku	[kuteks], [tʃat kuku]
hair spray	semprotan rambut	[semprotan rambut]
deodorant	deodoran	[deodoran]

cream	krim	[krim]
face cream	krim wajah	[krim wadʒ'ah]
hand cream	krim tangan	[krim taŋan]
anti-wrinkle cream	krim antikerut	[krim antikerut]
day cream	krim siang	[krim siaŋ]
night cream	krim malam	[krim malam]
day (as adj)	siang	[siaŋ]
night (as adj)	malam	[malam]

tampon	tampon	[tampon]
toilet paper (toilet roll)	kertas toilet	[kertas toylet]
hair dryer	pengering rambut	[peŋeriŋ rambut]

40. Watches. Clocks

watch (wristwatch)	arloji	[arlodʒi]
dial	piringan jam	[piriŋan dʒ'am]
hand (of clock, watch)	jarum	[dʒ'arum]
metal watch band	rantai arloji	[rantaj arlodʒi]
watch strap	tali arloji	[tali arlodʒi]

battery	baterai	[bateraj]
to be dead (battery)	mati	[mati]
to change a battery	mengganti baterai	[meŋganti bateraj]
to run fast	cepat	[tʃepat]

to run slow	**terlambat**	[tərlambat]
wall clock	**jam dinding**	[dʒّam dindiŋ]
hourglass	**jam pasir**	[dʒّam pasir]
sundial	**jam matahari**	[dʒّam matahari]
alarm clock	**weker**	[weker]
watchmaker	**tukang jam**	[tukaŋ dʒّam]
to repair (vt)	**mereparasi,** **memperbaiki**	[mereparasi], [memperbajki]

EVERYDAY EXPERIENCE

41. Money

money	**uang**	[uaŋ]
currency exchange	**pertukaran mata uang**	[pertukaran mata uaŋ]
exchange rate	**nilai tukar**	[nilaj tukar]
ATM	**Anjungan Tunai Mandiri, ATM**	[anʤʲuŋan tunaj mandiri], [a-te-em]
coin	**koin**	[koin]
dollar	**dolar**	[dolar]
euro	**euro**	[euro]
lira	**lira**	[lira]
Deutschmark	**Mark Jerman**	[marʔ ʤʲerman]
franc	**franc**	[franʧ]
pound sterling	**poundsterling**	[paundsterliŋ]
yen	**yen**	[yen]
debt	**utang**	[utaŋ]
debtor	**pengutang**	[peŋutaŋ]
to lend (money)	**meminjamkan**	[meminʤʲamkan]
to borrow (vi, vt)	**meminjam**	[meminʤʲam]
bank	**bank**	[banʔ]
account	**rekening**	[rekeniŋ]
to deposit (vt)	**memasukkan**	[memasuʔkan]
to deposit into the account	**memasukkan ke rekening**	[memasuʔkan ke rekeniŋ]
to withdraw (vt)	**menarik uang**	[menariʔ uaŋ]
credit card	**kartu kredit**	[kartu kredit]
cash	**uang kontan, uang tunai**	[uaŋ kontan], [uaŋ tunaj]
check	**cek**	[ʧeʔ]
to write a check	**menulis cek**	[menulis ʧeʔ]
checkbook	**buku cek**	[buku ʧeʔ]
wallet	**dompet**	[dompet]
change purse	**dompet, pundi-pundi**	[dompet], [pundi-pundi]
safe	**brankas**	[brankas]
heir	**pewaris**	[pewaris]
inheritance	**warisan**	[warisan]
fortune (wealth)	**kekayaan**	[kekajaʔan]
lease	**sewa**	[sewa]

rent (money)	**uang sewa**	[uaŋ sewa]
to rent (sth from sb)	**menyewa**	[mənjewa]
price	**harga**	[harga]
cost	**harga**	[harga]
sum	**jumlah**	[dʒˈumlah]
to spend (vt)	**menghabiskan**	[məŋhabiskan]
expenses	**ongkos**	[oŋkos]
to economize (vi, vt)	**menghemat**	[məɲhemat]
economical	**hemat**	[hemat]
to pay (vi, vt)	**membayar**	[membajar]
payment	**pembayaran**	[pembajaran]
change (give the ~)	**kembalian**	[kembalian]
tax	**pajak**	[padʒˈaʔ]
fine	**denda**	[denda]
to fine (vt)	**mendenda**	[mendenda]

42. Post. Postal service

post office	**kantor pos**	[kantor pos]
mail (letters, etc.)	**surat**	[surat]
mailman	**tukang pos**	[tukaŋ pos]
opening hours	**jam buka**	[dʒˈam buka]
letter	**surat**	[surat]
registered letter	**surat tercatat**	[surat tərtʃatat]
postcard	**kartu pos**	[kartu pos]
telegram	**telegram**	[telegram]
package (parcel)	**parsel, paket pos**	[parsel], [paket pos]
money transfer	**wesel pos**	[wesel pos]
to receive (vt)	**menerima**	[mənerima]
to send (vt)	**mengirim**	[məɲirim]
sending	**pengiriman**	[peɲiriman]
address	**alamat**	[alamat]
ZIP code	**kode pos**	[kode pos]
sender	**pengirim**	[peɲirim]
receiver	**penerima**	[penerima]
name (first name)	**nama**	[nama]
surname (last name)	**nama keluarga**	[nama keluarga]
postage rate	**tarif**	[tarif]
standard (adj)	**biasa, standar**	[biasa], [standar]
economical (adj)	**ekonomis**	[ekonomis]
weight	**berat**	[berat]

to weigh (~ letters)	menimbang	[mənimbaŋ]
envelope	amplop	[amplop]
postage stamp	prangko	[praŋko]
to stamp an envelope	menempelkan prangko	[mənempelkan praŋko]

43. Banking

bank	bank	[banˀ]
branch (of bank, etc.)	cabang	[ʧabaŋ]
bank clerk, consultant	konsultan	[konsultan]
manager (director)	manajer	[manadʒˈer]
bank account	rekening	[rekeniŋ]
account number	nomor rekening	[nomor rekeniŋ]
checking account	rekening koran	[rekeniŋ koran]
savings account	rekening simpanan	[rekeniŋ simpanan]
to open an account	membuka rekening	[membuka rekeniŋ]
to close the account	menutup rekening	[mənutup rekeniŋ]
to deposit into the account	memasukkan ke rekening	[memasuˀkan ke rekeniŋ]
to withdraw (vt)	menarik uang	[mənariˀ uaŋ]
deposit	deposito	[deposito]
to make a deposit	melakukan setoran	[melakukan setoran]
wire transfer	transfer kawat	[transfer kawat]
to wire, to transfer	mentransfer	[mentransfer]
sum	jumlah	[dʒˈumlah]
How much?	Berapa?	[bərapa?]
signature	tanda tangan	[tanda taŋan]
to sign (vt)	menandatangani	[mənandataŋani]
credit card	kartu kredit	[kartu kredit]
code (PIN code)	kode	[kode]
credit card number	nomor kartu kredit	[nomor kartu kredit]
ATM	Anjungan Tunai Mandiri, ATM	[andʒˈuŋan tunaj mandiri], [a-te-em]
check	cek	[ʧeˀ]
to write a check	menulis cek	[mənulis ʧeˀ]
checkbook	buku cek	[buku ʧeˀ]
loan (bank ~)	kredit, pinjaman	[kredit], [pindʒˈaman]
to apply for a loan	meminta kredit	[meminta kredit]
to get a loan	mendapatkan kredit	[məndapatkan kredit]
to give a loan	memberikan kredit	[memberikan kredit]
guarantee	jaminan	[dʒˈaminan]

44. Telephone. Phone conversation

telephone	**telepon**	[telepon]
cell phone	**ponsel**	[ponsel]
answering machine	**mesin penjawab panggilan**	[mesin pendʒ'awab paŋilan]
to call (by phone)	**menelepon**	[mənelepon]
phone call	**panggilan telepon**	[paŋilan telepon]
to dial a number	**memutar nomor telepon**	[memutar nomor telepon]
Hello!	**Halo!**	[halo!]
to ask (vt)	**bertanya**	[bertanja]
to answer (vi, vt)	**menjawab**	[məndʒ'awab]
to hear (vt)	**mendengar**	[məndeŋar]
well (adv)	**baik**	[baj']
not well (adv)	**buruk, jelek**	[buruk], [dʒ'ele']
noises (interference)	**bising, gangguan**	[bisiŋ], [gaŋguan]
receiver	**gagang**	[gagaŋ]
to pick up (~ the phone)	**mengangkat telepon**	[məŋaŋkat telepon]
to hang up (~ the phone)	**menutup telepon**	[mənutup telepon]
busy (engaged)	**sibuk**	[sibu']
to ring (ab. phone)	**berdering**	[berderiŋ]
telephone book	**buku telepon**	[buku telepon]
local (adj)	**lokal**	[lokal]
local call	**panggilan lokal**	[paŋilan lokal]
long distance (~ call)	**interlokal**	[interlokal]
long-distance call	**panggilan interlokal**	[paŋilan interlokal]
international (adj)	**internasional**	[internasional]
international call	**panggilan internasional**	[paŋilan internasional]

45. Cell phone

cell phone	**ponsel**	[ponsel]
display	**layar**	[lajar]
button	**kenop**	[kenop]
SIM card	**kartu SIM**	[kartu sim]
battery	**baterai**	[bateraj]
to be dead (battery)	**mati**	[mati]
charger	**pengisi baterai, pengecas**	[peŋisi bateraj], [peŋetʃas]
menu	**menu**	[menu]
settings	**penyetelan**	[penjetelan]

| tune (melody) | nada panggil | [nada paŋgil] |
| to select (vt) | memilih | [memilih] |

calculator	kalkulator	[kalkulator]
voice mail	penjawab telepon	[pendʒawab telepon]
alarm clock	weker	[weker]
contacts	buku telepon	[buku telepon]

| SMS (text message) | pesan singkat | [pesan siŋkat] |
| subscriber | pelanggan | [pelaŋgan] |

46. Stationery

| ballpoint pen | bolpen | [bolpen] |
| fountain pen | pena celup | [pena tʃelup] |

pencil	pensil	[pensil]
highlighter	spidol	[spidol]
felt-tip pen	spidol	[spidol]

| notepad | buku catatan | [buku tʃatatan] |
| agenda (diary) | agenda | [agenda] |

ruler	mistar, penggaris	[mistar], [peŋgaris]
calculator	kalkulator	[kalkulator]
eraser	karet penghapus	[karet peɲhapus]
thumbtack	paku payung	[paku pajuŋ]
paper clip	penjepit kertas	[pendʒepit kertas]

glue	lem	[lem]
stapler	stapler	[stapler]
hole punch	alat pelubang kertas	[alat pelubaŋ kertas]
pencil sharpener	rautan pensil	[rautan pensil]

47. Foreign languages

language	bahasa	[bahasa]
foreign (adj)	asing	[asiŋ]
foreign language	bahasa asing	[bahasa asiŋ]
to study (vt)	mempelajari	[mempeladʒari]
to learn (language, etc.)	belajar	[beladʒar]

to read (vi, vt)	membaca	[membatʃa]
to speak (vi, vt)	berbicara	[bərbitʃara]
to understand (vt)	mengerti	[məŋerti]
to write (vt)	menulis	[mənulis]
fast (adv)	cepat, fasih	[tʃepat], [fasih]
slowly (adv)	perlahan-lahan	[pərlahan-lahan]

fluently (adv)	**fasih**	[fasih]
rules	**peraturan**	[pəraturan]
grammar	**tatabahasa**	[tatabahasa]
vocabulary	**kosakata**	[kosakata]
phonetics	**fonetik**	[fonetiʔ]
textbook	**buku pelajaran**	[buku peladʒʲaran]
dictionary	**kamus**	[kamus]
teach-yourself book	**buku autodidak**	[buku autodidaʔ]
phrasebook	**panduan percakapan**	[panduan pərtʃakapan]
cassette, tape	**kaset**	[kaset]
videotape	**kaset video**	[kaset video]
CD, compact disc	**cakram kompak**	[tʃakram kompaʔ]
DVD	**cakram DVD**	[tʃakram di-vi-di]
alphabet	**alfabet, abjad**	[alfabet], [abdʒʲad]
to spell (vt)	**mengeja**	[məŋedʒʲa]
pronunciation	**pelafalan**	[pelafalan]
accent	**aksen**	[aksen]
with an accent	**dengan aksen**	[deŋan aksen]
without an accent	**tanpa aksen**	[tanpa aksen]
word	**kata**	[kata]
meaning	**arti**	[arti]
course (e.g., a French ~)	**kursus**	[kursus]
to sign up	**Mendaftar**	[məndaftar]
teacher	**guru**	[guru]
translation (process)	**penerjemahan**	[penerdʒʲemahan]
translation (text, etc.)	**terjemahan**	[tərdʒʲemahan]
translator	**penerjemah**	[penerdʒʲemah]
interpreter	**juru bahasa**	[dʒʲuru bahasa]
polyglot	**poliglot**	[poliglot]
memory	**memori, daya ingat**	[memori], [daja iŋat]

MEALS. RESTAURANT

48. Table setting

spoon	**sendok**	[sendoʔ]
knife	**pisau**	[pisau]
fork	**garpu**	[garpu]
cup (e.g., coffee ~)	**cangkir**	[tʃaŋkir]
plate (dinner ~)	**piring**	[piriŋ]
saucer	**alas cangkir**	[alas tʃaŋkir]
napkin (on table)	**serbet**	[serbet]
toothpick	**tusuk gigi**	[tusuʔ gigi]

49. Restaurant

restaurant	**restoran**	[restoran]
coffee house	**warung kopi**	[waruŋ kopi]
pub, bar	**bar**	[bar]
tearoom	**warung teh**	[waruŋ teh]
waiter	**pelayan lelaki**	[pelajan lelaki]
waitress	**pelayan perempuan**	[pelajan perempuan]
bartender	**pelayan bar**	[pelajan bar]
menu	**menu**	[menu]
wine list	**daftar anggur**	[daftar aŋgur]
to book a table	**memesan meja**	[memesan medʒʲa]
course, dish	**masakan, hidangan**	[masakan], [hidaŋan]
to order (meal)	**memesan**	[memesan]
to make an order	**memesan**	[memesan]
aperitif	**aperitif**	[aperitif]
appetizer	**makanan ringan**	[makanan riŋan]
dessert	**hidangan penutup**	[hidaŋan penutup]
check	**bon**	[bon]
to pay the check	**membayar bon**	[membajar bon]
to give change	**memberikan uang kembalian**	[memberikan uaŋ kembalian]
tip	**tip**	[tip]

50. Meals

food	**makanan**	[makanan]
to eat (vi, vt)	**makan**	[makan]
breakfast	**makan pagi, sarapan**	[makan pagi], [sarapan]
to have breakfast	**sarapan**	[sarapan]
lunch	**makan siang**	[makan siaŋ]
to have lunch	**makan siang**	[makan siaŋ]
dinner	**makan malam**	[makan malam]
to have dinner	**makan malam**	[makan malam]
appetite	**nafsu makan**	[nafsu makan]
Enjoy your meal!	**Selamat makan!**	[selamat makan!]
to open (~ a bottle)	**membuka**	[membuka]
to spill (liquid)	**menumpahkan**	[mənumpahkan]
to boil (vi)	**mendidih**	[məndidih]
to boil (vt)	**mendidihkan**	[məndidihkan]
boiled (~ water)	**masak**	[masaʔ]
to chill, cool down (vt)	**mendinginkan**	[məndiŋinkan]
to chill (vi)	**mendingin**	[məndiŋin]
taste, flavor	**rasa**	[rasa]
aftertaste	**nuansa rasa**	[nuansa rasa]
to slim down (lose weight)	**berdiet**	[berdiet]
diet	**diet, pola makan**	[diet], [pola makan]
vitamin	**vitamin**	[vitamin]
calorie	**kalori**	[kalori]
vegetarian (n)	**vegetarian**	[vegetarian]
vegetarian (adj)	**vegetarian**	[vegetarian]
fats (nutrient)	**lemak**	[lemaʔ]
proteins	**protein**	[protein]
carbohydrates	**karbohidrat**	[karbohidrat]
slice (of lemon, ham)	**irisan**	[irisan]
piece (of cake, pie)	**potongan**	[potoŋan]
crumb (of bread, cake, etc.)	**remah**	[remah]

51. Cooked dishes

course, dish	**masakan, hidangan**	[masakan], [hidaŋan]
cuisine	**masakan**	[masakan]
recipe	**resep**	[resep]
portion	**porsi**	[porsi]

| salad | **salada** | [salada] |
| soup | **sup** | [sup] |

clear soup (broth)	**kaldu**	[kaldu]
sandwich (bread)	**roti lapis**	[roti lapis]
fried eggs	**telur mata sapi**	[telur mata sapi]

| hamburger (beefburger) | **hamburger** | [hamburger] |
| beefsteak | **bistik** | [bistiʔ] |

side dish	**lauk**	[lauʔ]
spaghetti	**spageti**	[spageti]
mashed potatoes	**kentang tumbuk**	[kentaŋ tumbuʔ]
pizza	**piza**	[piza]
porridge (oatmeal, etc.)	**bubur**	[bubur]
omelet	**telur dadar**	[telur dadar]

boiled (e.g., ~ beef)	**rebus**	[rebus]
smoked (adj)	**asap**	[asap]
fried (adj)	**goreng**	[goreŋ]
dried (adj)	**kering**	[keriŋ]
frozen (adj)	**beku**	[beku]
pickled (adj)	**marinade**	[marinade]

sweet (sugary)	**manis**	[manis]
salty (adj)	**asin**	[asin]
cold (adj)	**dingin**	[diŋin]
hot (adj)	**panas**	[panas]
bitter (adj)	**pahit**	[pahit]
tasty (adj)	**enak**	[enaʔ]

to cook in boiling water	**merebus**	[merebus]
to cook (dinner)	**memasak**	[memasaʔ]
to fry (vt)	**menggoreng**	[meŋgoreŋ]
to heat up (food)	**memanaskan**	[memanaskan]

to salt (vt)	**menggarami**	[meŋgarami]
to pepper (vt)	**membubuh merica**	[membubuh meritʃa]
to grate (vt)	**memarut**	[memarut]
peel (n)	**kulit**	[kulit]
to peel (vt)	**mengupas**	[meŋupas]

52. Food

meat	**daging**	[dagiŋ]
chicken	**ayam**	[ajam]
Rock Cornish hen (poussin)	**anak ayam**	[anaʔ ajam]
duck	**bebek**	[bebeʔ]
goose	**angsa**	[aŋsa]

| game | binatang buruan | [binataŋ buruan] |
| turkey | kalkun | [kalkun] |

pork	daging babi	[dagiŋ babi]
veal	daging anak sapi	[dagiŋ ana' sapi]
lamb	daging domba	[dagiŋ domba]
beef	daging sapi	[dagiŋ sapi]
rabbit	kelinci	[kelintʃi]

sausage (bologna, pepperoni, etc.)	sosis	[sosis]
vienna sausage (frankfurter)	sosis	[sosis]
bacon	bakon	[beykon]
ham	ham, daging kornet	[ham], [dagiŋ kornet]
gammon	ham	[ham]

pâté	pasta	[pasta]
liver	hati	[hati]
hamburger (ground beef)	daging giling	[dagiŋ giliŋ]
tongue	lidah	[lidah]

egg	telur	[telur]
eggs	telur	[telur]
egg white	putih telur	[putih telur]
egg yolk	kuning telur	[kuniŋ telur]

fish	ikan	[ikan]
seafood	makanan laut	[makanan laut]
crustaceans	krustasea	[krustasea]
caviar	caviar	[kaviar]

crab	kepiting	[kepitiŋ]
shrimp	udang	[udaŋ]
oyster	tiram	[tiram]
spiny lobster	lobster berduri	[lobster berduri]
octopus	gurita	[gurita]
squid	cumi-cumi	[tʃumi-tʃumi]

sturgeon	ikan sturgeon	[ikan sturdʒʲen]
salmon	salmon	[salmon]
halibut	ikan turbot	[ikan turbot]

cod	ikan kod	[ikan kod]
mackerel	ikan kembung	[ikan kembuŋ]
tuna	tuna	[tuna]
eel	belut	[belut]

trout	ikan forel	[ikan forel]
sardine	sarden	[sarden]
pike	ikan pike	[ikan paik]
herring	ikan haring	[ikan hariŋ]

bread	**roti**	[roti]
cheese	**keju**	[kedʒⁱu]
sugar	**gula**	[gula]
salt	**garam**	[garam]

rice	**beras, nasi**	[beras], [nasi]
pasta (macaroni)	**makaroni**	[makaroni]
noodles	**mi**	[mi]

butter	**mentega**	[məntega]
vegetable oil	**minyak nabati**	[minja' nabati]
sunflower oil	**minyak bunga matahari**	[minja' buŋa matahari]
margarine	**margarin**	[margarin]

| olives | **buah zaitun** | [buah zajtun] |
| olive oil | **minyak zaitun** | [minja' zajtun] |

milk	**susu**	[susu]
condensed milk	**susu kental**	[susu kental]
yogurt	**yogurt**	[yogurt]
sour cream	**krim asam**	[krim asam]
cream (of milk)	**krim, kepala susu**	[krim], [kepala susu]

| mayonnaise | **mayones** | [majones] |
| buttercream | **krim** | [krim] |

cereal grains (wheat, etc.)	**menir**	[menir]
flour	**tepung**	[tepuŋ]
canned food	**makanan kalengan**	[makanan kaleŋan]

cornflakes	**emping jagung**	[empiŋ dʒⁱaguŋ]
honey	**madu**	[madu]
jam	**selai**	[selaj]
chewing gum	**permen karet**	[permen karet]

53. Drinks

water	**air**	[air]
drinking water	**air minum**	[air minum]
mineral water	**air mineral**	[air mineral]

still (adj)	**tanpa gas**	[tanpa gas]
carbonated (adj)	**berkarbonasi**	[berkarbonasi]
sparkling (adj)	**bergas**	[bergas]
ice	**es**	[es]
with ice	**dengan es**	[deŋan es]

non-alcoholic (adj)	**tanpa alkohol**	[tanpa alkohol]
soft drink	**minuman ringan**	[minuman riŋan]
refreshing drink	**minuman penygar**	[minuman penigar]

lemonade	**limun**	[limun]
liquors	**minoman beralkohol**	[minoman bəralkohol]
wine	**anggur**	[aŋgur]
white wine	**anggur putih**	[aŋgur putih]
red wine	**anggur merah**	[aŋgur merah]
liqueur	**likeur**	[likeur]
champagne	**sampanye**	[sampanje]
vermouth	**vermouth**	[vermut]
whiskey	**wiski**	[wiski]
vodka	**vodka**	[vodka]
gin	**jin, jenewer**	[dʒin], [dʒ'enewer]
cognac	**konyak**	[konjaʔ]
rum	**rum**	[rum]
coffee	**kopi**	[kopi]
black coffee	**kopi pahit**	[kopi pahit]
coffee with milk	**kopi susu**	[kopi susu]
cappuccino	**cappuccino**	[kaputʃino]
instant coffee	**kopi instan**	[kopi instan]
milk	**susu**	[susu]
cocktail	**koktail**	[koktajl]
milkshake	**susu kocok**	[susu kotʃoʔ]
juice	**jus**	[dʒ'us]
tomato juice	**jus tomat**	[dʒ'us tomat]
orange juice	**jus jeruk**	[dʒ'us dʒ'eruʔ]
freshly squeezed juice	**jus peras**	[dʒ'us pəras]
beer	**bir**	[bir]
light beer	**bir putih**	[bir putih]
dark beer	**bir hitam**	[bir hitam]
tea	**teh**	[teh]
black tea	**teh hitam**	[teh hitam]
green tea	**teh hijau**	[teh hidʒ'au]

54. Vegetables

vegetables	**sayuran**	[sajuran]
greens	**sayuran hijau**	[sajuran hidʒ'au]
tomato	**tomat**	[tomat]
cucumber	**mentimun, ketimun**	[məntimun], [ketimun]
carrot	**wortel**	[wortel]
potato	**kentang**	[kentaŋ]
onion	**bawang**	[bawaŋ]
garlic	**bawang putih**	[bawaŋ putih]

cabbage	**kol**	[kol]
cauliflower	**kembang kol**	[kembaŋ kol]
Brussels sprouts	**kol Brussels**	[kol brusels]
broccoli	**brokoli**	[brokoli]

beetroot	**ubi bit merah**	[ubi bit merah]
eggplant	**terung, terong**	[teruŋ], [teroŋ]
zucchini	**labu siam**	[labu siam]
pumpkin	**labu**	[labu]
turnip	**turnip**	[turnip]

parsley	**peterseli**	[peterseli]
dill	**adas sowa**	[adas sowa]
lettuce	**selada**	[selada]
celery	**seledri**	[seledri]
asparagus	**asparagus**	[asparagus]
spinach	**bayam**	[bajam]

pea	**kacang polong**	[katʃaŋ poloŋ]
beans	**kacang-kacangan**	[katʃaŋ-katʃaŋan]
corn (maize)	**jagung**	[dʒʲaguŋ]
kidney bean	**kacang buncis**	[katʃaŋ buntʃis]

bell pepper	**cabai**	[tʃabaj]
radish	**radis**	[radis]
artichoke	**artisyok**	[artiʃoʔ]

55. Fruits. Nuts

fruit	**buah**	[buah]
apple	**apel**	[apel]
pear	**pir**	[pir]
lemon	**jeruk sitrun**	[dʒʲeruʔ sitrun]
orange	**jeruk manis**	[dʒʲeruʔ manis]
strawberry (garden ~)	**stroberi**	[stroberi]

mandarin	**jeruk mandarin**	[dʒʲeruʔ mandarin]
plum	**plum**	[plum]
peach	**persik**	[persiʔ]
apricot	**aprikot**	[aprikot]
raspberry	**buah frambus**	[buah frambus]
pineapple	**nanas**	[nanas]

banana	**pisang**	[pisaŋ]
watermelon	**semangka**	[semaŋka]
grape	**buah anggur**	[buah aŋgur]
sour cherry	**buah ceri asam**	[buah tʃeri asam]
sweet cherry	**buah ceri manis**	[buah tʃeri manis]
melon	**melon**	[melon]
grapefruit	**jeruk Bali**	[dʒʲeruʔ bali]

avocado	**avokad**	[avokad]
papaya	**pepaya**	[pepaja]
mango	**mangga**	[maŋga]
pomegranate	**buah delima**	[buah delima]

redcurrant	**redcurrant**	[redkaren]
blackcurrant	**blackcurrant**	[bleʔkaren]
gooseberry	**buah arbei hijau**	[buah arbei hidʒau]
bilberry	**buah bilberi**	[buah bilberi]
blackberry	**beri hitam**	[beri hitam]

raisin	**kismis**	[kismis]
fig	**buah ara**	[buah ara]
date	**buah kurma**	[buah kurma]

peanut	**kacang tanah**	[katʃaŋ tanah]
almond	**badam**	[badam]
walnut	**buah walnut**	[buah walnut]
hazelnut	**kacang hazel**	[katʃaŋ hazel]
coconut	**buah kelapa**	[buah kelapa]
pistachios	**badam hijau**	[badam hidʒau]

56. Bread. Candy

bakers' confectionery (pastry)	**kue-mue**	[kue-mue]
bread	**roti**	[roti]
cookies	**biskuit**	[biskuit]

chocolate (n)	**cokelat**	[tʃokelat]
chocolate (as adj)	**cokelat**	[tʃokelat]
candy (wrapped)	**permen**	[permen]
cake (e.g., cupcake)	**kue**	[kue]
cake (e.g., birthday ~)	**kue tar**	[kue tar]

| pie (e.g., apple ~) | **pai** | [pai] |
| filling (for cake, pie) | **inti** | [inti] |

jam (whole fruit jam)	**selai buah utuh**	[selaj buah utuh]
marmalade	**marmelade**	[marmelade]
waffles	**wafel**	[wafel]
ice-cream	**es krim**	[es krim]
pudding	**puding**	[pudiŋ]

57. Spices

| salt | **garam** | [garam] |
| salty (adj) | **asin** | [asin] |

to salt (vt)	**menggarami**	[məŋgarami]
black pepper	**merica**	[meritʃa]
red pepper (milled ~)	**cabai merah**	[tʃabaj merah]
mustard	**mustar**	[mustar]
horseradish	**lobak pedas**	[loba' pedas]
condiment	**bumbu**	[bumbu]
spice	**rempah-rempah**	[rempah-rempah]
sauce	**saus**	[saus]
vinegar	**cuka**	[tʃuka]
anise	**adas manis**	[adas manis]
basil	**selasih**	[selasih]
cloves	**cengkih**	[tʃeŋkih]
ginger	**jahe**	[dʒʲahe]
coriander	**ketumbar**	[ketumbar]
cinnamon	**kayu manis**	[kaju manis]
sesame	**wijen**	[widʒʲen]
bay leaf	**daun salam**	[daun salam]
paprika	**cabai**	[tʃabaj]
caraway	**jintan**	[dʒintan]
saffron	**kuma-kuma**	[kuma-kuma]

PERSONAL INFORMATION. FAMILY

58. Personal information. Forms

name (first name)	**nama, nama depan**	[nama], [nama depan]
surname (last name)	**nama keluarga**	[nama keluarga]
date of birth	**tanggal lahir**	[taŋgal lahir]
place of birth	**tempat lahir**	[tempat lahir]
nationality	**kebangsaan**	[kebaŋsa'an]
place of residence	**tempat tinggal**	[tempat tiŋgal]
country	**negara, negeri**	[negara], [negeri]
profession (occupation)	**profesi**	[profesi]
gender, sex	**jenis kelamin**	[dʒ'enis kelamin]
height	**tinggi badan**	[tiŋgi badan]
weight	**berat**	[berat]

59. Family members. Relatives

mother	**ibu**	[ibu]
father	**ayah**	[ajah]
son	**anak lelaki**	[ana' lelaki]
daughter	**anak perempuan**	[ana' perempuan]
younger daughter	**anak perempuan bungsu**	[ana' perempuan buŋsu]
younger son	**anak lelaki bungsu**	[ana' lelaki buŋsu]
eldest daughter	**anak perempuan sulung**	[ana' perempuan suluŋ]
eldest son	**anak lelaki sulung**	[ana' lelaki suluŋ]
brother	**saudara lelaki**	[saudara lelaki]
elder brother	**kakak lelaki**	[kaka' lelaki]
younger brother	**adik lelaki**	[adi' lelaki]
sister	**saudara perempuan**	[saudara perempuan]
elder sister	**kakak perempuan**	[kaka' perempuan]
younger sister	**adik perempuan**	[adi' perempuan]
cousin (masc.)	**sepupu lelaki**	[sepupu lelaki]
cousin (fem.)	**sepupu perempuan**	[sepupu perempuan]
mom, mommy	**mama, ibu**	[mama], [ibu]
dad, daddy	**papa, ayah**	[papa], [ajah]
parents	**orang tua**	[oraŋ tua]
child	**anak**	[ana']
children	**anak-anak**	[ana'-ana']

grandmother	**nenek**	[neneʔ]
grandfather	**kakek**	[kakeʔ]
grandson	**cucu laki-laki**	[ʧuʧu laki-laki]
granddaughter	**cucu perempuan**	[ʧuʧu pərempuan]
grandchildren	**cucu**	[ʧuʧu]
uncle	**paman**	[paman]
aunt	**bibi**	[bibi]
nephew	**keponakan laki-laki**	[keponakan laki-laki]
niece	**keponakan perempuan**	[keponakan pərempuan]
mother-in-law (wife's mother)	**ibu mertua**	[ibu mertua]
father-in-law (husband's father)	**ayah mertua**	[ajah mertua]
son-in-law (daughter's husband)	**menantu laki-laki**	[mənantu laki-laki]
stepmother	**ibu tiri**	[ibu tiri]
stepfather	**ayah tiri**	[ajah tiri]
infant	**bayi**	[baji]
baby (infant)	**bayi**	[baji]
little boy, kid	**bocah cilik**	[botʃah ʧiliʔ]
wife	**istri**	[istri]
husband	**suami**	[suami]
spouse (husband)	**suami**	[suami]
spouse (wife)	**istri**	[istri]
married (masc.)	**menikah, beristri**	[mənikah], [bəristri]
married (fem.)	**menikah, bersuami**	[mənikah], [bərsuami]
single (unmarried)	**bujang**	[buʤʲaŋ]
bachelor	**bujang**	[buʤʲaŋ]
divorced (masc.)	**bercerai**	[bərtʃeraj]
widow	**janda**	[ʤʲanda]
widower	**duda**	[duda]
relative	**kerabat**	[kerabat]
close relative	**kerabat dekat**	[kerabat dekat]
distant relative	**kerabat jauh**	[kerabat ʤʲauh]
relatives	**kerabat, sanak saudara**	[kerabat], [sanaʔ saudara]
orphan (boy or girl)	**yatim piatu**	[yatim piatu]
guardian (of a minor)	**wali**	[wali]
to adopt (a boy)	**mengadopsi**	[məŋadopsi]
to adopt (a girl)	**mengadopsi**	[məŋadopsi]

60. Friends. Coworkers

friend (masc.)	**sahabat**	[sahabat]
friend (fem.)	**sahabat**	[sahabat]

| friendship | **persahabatan** | [pərsahabatan] |
| to be friends | **bersahabat** | [bərsahabat] |

buddy (masc.)	**teman**	[teman]
buddy (fem.)	**teman**	[teman]
partner	**mitra**	[mitra]

chief (boss)	**atasan**	[atasan]
superior (n)	**atasan**	[atasan]
owner, proprietor	**pemilik**	[pemili']
subordinate (n)	**bawahan**	[bawahan]
colleague	**kolega**	[kolega]

acquaintance (person)	**kenalan**	[kenalan]
fellow traveler	**rekan seperjalanan**	[rekan seperdʒʲalanan]
classmate	**teman sekelas**	[teman sekelas]

neighbor (masc.)	**tetangga**	[tetaŋga]
neighbor (fem.)	**tetangga**	[tetaŋga]
neighbors	**para tetangga**	[para tetaŋga]

HUMAN BODY. MEDICINE

61. Head

head	**kepala**	[kepala]
face	**wajah**	[wadʒ'ah]
nose	**hidung**	[hiduŋ]
mouth	**mulut**	[mulut]
eye	**mata**	[mata]
eyes	**mata**	[mata]
pupil	**pupil, biji mata**	[pupil], [bidʒi mata]
eyebrow	**alis**	[alis]
eyelash	**bulu mata**	[bulu mata]
eyelid	**kelopak mata**	[kelopa' mata]
tongue	**lidah**	[lidah]
tooth	**gigi**	[gigi]
lips	**bibir**	[bibir]
cheekbones	**tulang pipi**	[tulaŋ pipi]
gum	**gusi**	[gusi]
palate	**langit-langit mulut**	[laŋit-laŋit mulut]
nostrils	**lubang hidung**	[lubaŋ hiduŋ]
chin	**dagu**	[dagu]
jaw	**rahang**	[rahaŋ]
cheek	**pipi**	[pipi]
forehead	**dahi**	[dahi]
temple	**pelipis**	[pelipis]
ear	**telinga**	[teliŋa]
back of the head	**tengkuk**	[teŋku']
neck	**leher**	[leher]
throat	**tenggorok**	[teŋgoro']
hair	**rambut**	[rambut]
hairstyle	**tatanan rambut**	[tatanan rambut]
haircut	**potongan rambut**	[potoŋan rambut]
wig	**wig, rambut palsu**	[wig], [rambut palsu]
mustache	**kumis**	[kumis]
beard	**janggut**	[dʒ'aŋgut]
to have (a beard, etc.)	**memelihara**	[memelihara]
braid	**kepang**	[kepaŋ]
sideburns	**brewok**	[brewo']
red-haired (adj)	**merah pirang**	[merah piraŋ]

gray (hair)	beruban	[bəruban]
bald (adj)	botak, plontos	[botak], [plontos]
bald patch	botak	[botaʔ]

| ponytail | ekor kuda | [ekor kuda] |
| bangs | poni rambut | [poni rambut] |

62. Human body

| hand | tangan | [taŋan] |
| arm | lengan | [leŋan] |

finger	jari	[dʒʲari]
toe	jari	[dʒʲari]
thumb	jempol	[dʒʲempol]
little finger	jari kelingking	[dʒʲari keliŋkiŋ]
nail	kuku	[kuku]

fist	kepalan tangan	[kepalan taŋan]
palm	telapak	[telapaʔ]
wrist	pergelangan	[pərgelaŋan]
forearm	lengan bawah	[leŋan bawah]
elbow	siku	[siku]
shoulder	bahu	[bahu]

leg	kaki	[kaki]
foot	telapak kaki	[telapaʔ kaki]
knee	lutut	[lutut]
calf (part of leg)	betis	[betis]
hip	paha	[paha]
heel	tumit	[tumit]

body	tubuh	[tubuh]
stomach	perut	[perut]
chest	dada	[dada]
breast	payudara	[pajudara]
flank	rusuk	[rusuʔ]
back	punggung	[puŋguŋ]
lower back	pinggang bawah	[piŋgan bawah]
waist	pinggang	[piŋgan]

navel (belly button)	pusar	[pusar]
buttocks	pantat	[pantat]
bottom	pantat	[pantat]

beauty mark	tanda lahir	[tanda lahir]
birthmark (café au lait spot)	tanda lahir	[tanda lahir]
tattoo	tato	[tato]
scar	parut luka	[parut luka]

63. Diseases

sickness	**penyakit**	[peɲakit]
to be sick	**sakit**	[sakit]
health	**kesehatan**	[kesehatan]
runny nose (coryza)	**hidung meler**	[hiduŋ meler]
tonsillitis	**radang tonsil**	[radaŋ tonsil]
cold (illness)	**pilek, selesma**	[pilek], [selesma]
to catch a cold	**masuk angin**	[masuʔ aŋin]
bronchitis	**bronkitis**	[bronkitis]
pneumonia	**radang paru-paru**	[radaŋ paru-paru]
flu, influenza	**flu**	[flu]
nearsighted (adj)	**rabun jauh**	[rabun dʒˈauh]
farsighted (adj)	**rabun dekat**	[rabun dekat]
strabismus (crossed eyes)	**mata juling**	[mata dʒˈuliŋ]
cross-eyed (adj)	**bermata juling**	[bərmata dʒˈuliŋ]
cataract	**katarak**	[kataraʔ]
glaucoma	**glaukoma**	[glaukoma]
stroke	**stroke**	[stroke]
heart attack	**infark**	[infarʔ]
myocardial infarction	**serangan jantung**	[seraŋan dʒˈantuŋ]
paralysis	**kelumpuhan**	[kelumpuhan]
to paralyze (vt)	**melumpuhkan**	[melumpuhkan]
allergy	**alergi**	[alergi]
asthma	**asma**	[asma]
diabetes	**diabetes**	[diabetes]
toothache	**sakit gigi**	[sakit gigi]
caries	**karies**	[karies]
diarrhea	**diare**	[diare]
constipation	**konstipasi, sembelit**	[konstipasi], [sembelit]
stomach upset	**gangguan pencernaan**	[gaŋuan pentʃarna'an]
food poisoning	**keracunan makanan**	[keratʃunan makanan]
to get food poisoning	**keracunan makanan**	[keratʃunan makanan]
arthritis	**artritis**	[artritis]
rickets	**rakitis**	[rakitis]
rheumatism	**rematik**	[remati']
atherosclerosis	**aterosklerosis**	[aterosklerosis]
gastritis	**radang perut**	[radaŋ perut]
appendicitis	**apendisitis**	[apendisitis]
cholecystitis	**radang pundi empedu**	[radaŋ pundi empedu]
ulcer	**tukak lambung**	[tukaʔ lambuŋ]
measles	**penyakit campak**	[peɲakit tʃampaʔ]

rubella (German measles)	**penyakit campak Jerman**	[penjakit tʃampaʔ dʒʲerman]
jaundice	**sakit kuning**	[sakit kuniŋ]
hepatitis	**hepatitis**	[hepatitis]
schizophrenia	**skizofrenia**	[skizofrenia]
rabies (hydrophobia)	**rabies**	[rabies]
neurosis	**neurosis**	[neurosis]
concussion	**gegar otak**	[gegar otaʔ]
cancer	**kanker**	[kanker]
sclerosis	**sklerosis**	[sklerosis]
multiple sclerosis	**sklerosis multipel**	[sklerosis multipel]
alcoholism	**alkoholisme**	[alkoholisme]
alcoholic (n)	**alkoholik**	[alkoholiʔ]
syphilis	**sifilis**	[sifilis]
AIDS	**AIDS**	[ajds]
tumor	**tumor**	[tumor]
malignant (adj)	**ganas**	[ganas]
benign (adj)	**jinak**	[dʒinaʔ]
fever	**demam**	[demam]
malaria	**malaria**	[malaria]
gangrene	**gangren**	[gaŋren]
seasickness	**mabuk laut**	[mabuʔ laut]
epilepsy	**epilepsi**	[epilepsi]
epidemic	**epidemi**	[epidemi]
typhus	**tifus**	[tifus]
tuberculosis	**tuberkulosis**	[tuberkulosis]
cholera	**kolera**	[kolera]
plague (bubonic ~)	**penyakit pes**	[penjakit pes]

64. Symptoms. Treatments. Part 1

symptom	**gejala**	[gedʒʲala]
temperature	**temperatur, suhu**	[temperatur], [suhu]
high temperature (fever)	**temperatur tinggi**	[temperatur tiŋgi]
pulse	**denyut nadi**	[denyut nadi]
dizziness (vertigo)	**rasa pening**	[rasa peniŋ]
hot (adj)	**panas**	[panas]
shivering	**menggigil**	[meŋgigil]
pale (e.g., ~ face)	**pucat**	[putʃat]
cough	**batuk**	[batuʔ]
to cough (vi)	**batuk**	[batuʔ]
to sneeze (vi)	**bersin**	[bersin]
faint	**pingsan**	[piŋsan]

to faint (vi)	**jatuh pingsan**	[dʒatuh piŋsan]
bruise (hématome)	**luka memar**	[luka memar]
bump (lump)	**bengkak**	[beŋkaʔ]
to bang (bump)	**terantuk**	[tərantuʔ]
contusion (bruise)	**luka memar**	[luka memar]
to get a bruise	**kena luka memar**	[kena luka memar]
to limp (vi)	**pincang**	[pintʃaŋ]
dislocation	**keseleo**	[keseleo]
to dislocate (vt)	**keseleo**	[keseleo]
fracture	**fraktura, patah tulang**	[fraktura], [patah tulaŋ]
to have a fracture	**patah tulang**	[patah tulaŋ]
cut (e.g., paper ~)	**teriris**	[təriris]
to cut oneself	**teriris**	[təriris]
bleeding	**perdarahan**	[pərdarahan]
burn (injury)	**luka bakar**	[luka bakar]
to get burned	**menderita luka bakar**	[məndərita luka bakar]
to prick (vt)	**menusuk**	[mənusuʔ]
to prick oneself	**tertusuk**	[tərtusuʔ]
to injure (vt)	**melukai**	[melukaj]
injury	**cedera**	[tʃedera]
wound	**luka**	[luka]
trauma	**trauma**	[trauma]
to be delirious	**mengigau**	[məŋigau]
to stutter (vi)	**gagap**	[gagap]
sunstroke	**sengatan matahari**	[seŋatan matahari]

65. Symptoms. Treatments. Part 2

pain, ache	**sakit**	[sakit]
splinter (in foot, etc.)	**selumbar**	[selumbar]
sweat (perspiration)	**keringat**	[keriŋat]
to sweat (perspire)	**berkeringat**	[bərkeriŋat]
vomiting	**muntah**	[muntah]
convulsions	**kram**	[kram]
pregnant (adj)	**hamil**	[hamil]
to be born	**lahir**	[lahir]
delivery, labor	**persalinan**	[persalinan]
to deliver (~ a baby)	**melahirkan**	[melahirkan]
abortion	**aborsi**	[aborsi]
breathing, respiration	**pernapasan**	[pernapasan]
in-breath (inhalation)	**tarikan napas**	[tarikan napas]
out-breath (exhalation)	**napas keluar**	[napas keluar]

| to exhale (breathe out) | mengembuskan napas | [mənembuskan napas] |
| to inhale (vi) | menarik napas | [mənari' napas] |

disabled person	penderita cacat	[penderita tʃatʃat]
cripple	penderita cacat	[penderita tʃatʃat]
drug addict	pecandu narkoba	[petʃandu narkoba]

deaf (adj)	tunarungu	[tunaruŋu]
mute (adj)	tunawicara	[tunawitʃara]
deaf mute (adj)	tunarungu-wicara	[tunaruŋu-witʃara]

mad, insane (adj)	gila	[gila]
madman (demented person)	lelaki gila	[lelaki gila]
madwoman	perempuan gila	[pərempuan gila]
to go insane	menggila	[məŋgila]

gene	gen	[gen]
immunity	imunitas	[imunitas]
hereditary (adj)	turun-temurun	[turun-temurun]
congenital (adj)	bawaan	[bawa'an]

virus	virus	[virus]
microbe	mikroba	[mikroba]
bacterium	bakteri	[bakteri]
infection	infeksi	[infeksi]

66. Symptoms. Treatments. Part 3

| hospital | rumah sakit | [rumah sakit] |
| patient | pasien | [pasien] |

diagnosis	diagnosis	[diagnosis]
cure	perawatan	[pərawatan]
medical treatment	pengobatan medis	[pəŋobatan medis]
to get treatment	berobat	[bərobat]
to treat (~ a patient)	merawat	[merawat]
to nurse (look after)	merawat	[merawat]
care (nursing ~)	pengasuhan	[pəŋasuhan]

operation, surgery	operasi, pembedahan	[operasi], [pembedahan]
to bandage (head, limb)	membalut	[membalut]
bandaging	pembalutan	[pembalutan]

vaccination	vaksinasi	[vaksinasi]
to vaccinate (vt)	memvaksinasi	[memvaksinasi]
injection, shot	suntikan	[suntikan]
to give an injection	menyuntik	[mənyunti']
attack	serangan	[seraŋan]
amputation	amputasi	[amputasi]

to amputate (vt)	mengamputasi	[məɲamputasi]
coma	koma	[koma]
to be in a coma	dalam keadaan koma	[dalam keada'an koma]
intensive care	perawatan intensif	[pərawatan intensif]
to recover (~ from flu)	sembuh	[sembuh]
condition (patient's ~)	keadaan	[keada'an]
consciousness	kesadaran	[kesadaran]
memory (faculty)	memori, daya ingat	[memori], [daja iŋat]
to pull out (tooth)	mencabut	[məntʃabut]
filling	tambalan	[tambalan]
to fill (a tooth)	menambal	[mənambal]
hypnosis	hipnosis	[hipnosis]
to hypnotize (vt)	menghipnosis	[məɲhipnosis]

67. Medicine. Drugs. Accessories

medicine, drug	obat	[obat]
remedy	obat	[obat]
to prescribe (vt)	meresepkan	[meresepkan]
prescription	resep	[resep]
tablet, pill	pil, tablet	[pil], [tablet]
ointment	salep	[salep]
ampule	ampul	[ampul]
mixture	obat cair	[obat tʃajr]
syrup	sirop	[sirop]
pill	pil	[pil]
powder	bubuk	[bubu']
gauze bandage	perban	[perban]
cotton wool	kapas	[kapas]
iodine	iodium	[iodium]
Band-Aid	plester obat	[plester obat]
eyedropper	tetes mata	[tetes mata]
thermometer	termometer	[tərmometər]
syringe	alat suntik	[alat sunti']
wheelchair	kursi roda	[kursi roda]
crutches	kruk	[kru']
painkiller	obat bius	[obat bius]
laxative	laksatif, obat pencuci perut	[laksatif], [obat pentʃutʃi pərut]
spirits (ethanol)	spiritus, alkohol	[spiritus], [alkohol]
medicinal herbs	tanaman obat	[tanaman obat]
herbal (~ tea)	herbal	[herbal]

APARTMENT

68. Apartment

apartment	**apartemen**	[apartemen]
room	**kamar**	[kamar]
bedroom	**kamar tidur**	[kamar tidur]
dining room	**ruang makan**	[ruaŋ makan]
living room	**ruang tamu**	[ruaŋ tamu]
study (home office)	**ruang kerja**	[ruaŋ kerdʒ'a]
entry room	**ruang depan**	[ruaŋ depan]
bathroom (room with a bath or shower)	**kamar mandi**	[kamar mandi]
half bath	**kamar kecil**	[kamar ketʃil]
ceiling	**plafon, langit-langit**	[plafon], [laŋit-laŋit]
floor	**lantai**	[lantaj]
corner	**sudut**	[sudut]

69. Furniture. Interior

furniture	**mebel**	[mebel]
table	**meja**	[medʒ'a]
chair	**kursi**	[kursi]
bed	**ranjang**	[randʒ'aŋ]
couch, sofa	**dipan**	[dipan]
armchair	**kursi malas**	[kursi malas]
bookcase	**lemari buku**	[lemari buku]
shelf	**rak**	[raʔ]
wardrobe	**lemari pakaian**	[lemari pakajan]
coat rack (wall-mounted ~)	**kapstok**	[kapstoʔ]
coat stand	**kapstok berdiri**	[kapstoʔ bərdiri]
bureau, dresser	**lemari laci**	[lemari latʃi]
coffee table	**meja kopi**	[medʒ'a kopi]
mirror	**cermin**	[tʃermin]
carpet	**permadani**	[pərmadani]
rug, small carpet	**karpet kecil**	[karpet ketʃil]
fireplace	**perapian**	[pərapian]
candle	**lilin**	[lilin]

candlestick	**kaki lilin**	[kaki lilin]
drapes	**gorden**	[gorden]
wallpaper	**kertas dinding**	[kertas dindiŋ]
blinds (jalousie)	**kerai**	[keraj]

table lamp	**lampu meja**	[lampu medʒʲa]
wall lamp (sconce)	**lampu dinding**	[lampu dindiŋ]
floor lamp	**lampu lantai**	[lampu lantaj]
chandelier	**lampu bercabang**	[lampu bertʃabaŋ]

leg (of chair, table)	**kaki**	[kaki]
armrest	**lengan**	[leŋan]
back (backrest)	**sandaran**	[sandaran]
drawer	**laci**	[latʃi]

70. Bedding

bedclothes	**kain kasur**	[kain kasur]
pillow	**bantal**	[bantal]
pillowcase	**sarung bantal**	[saruŋ bantal]
duvet, comforter	**selimut**	[selimut]
sheet	**seprai**	[sepraj]
bedspread	**selubung kasur**	[selubuŋ kasur]

71. Kitchen

kitchen	**dapur**	[dapur]
gas	**gas**	[gas]
gas stove (range)	**kompor gas**	[kompor gas]
electric stove	**kompor listrik**	[kompor listriʔ]
oven	**oven**	[oven]
microwave oven	**microwave**	[majkrowav]

refrigerator	**lemari es, kulkas**	[lemari es], [kulkas]
freezer	**lemari pembeku**	[lemari pembeku]
dishwasher	**mesin pencuci piring**	[mesin pentʃutʃi piriŋ]

meat grinder	**alat pelumat daging**	[alat pelumat dagiŋ]
juicer	**mesin sari buah**	[mesin sari buah]
toaster	**alat pemanggang roti**	[alat pemaŋgaŋ roti]
mixer	**pencampur**	[pentʃampur]

coffee machine	**mesin pembuat kopi**	[mesin pembuat kopi]
coffee pot	**teko kopi**	[teko kopi]
coffee grinder	**mesin penggiling kopi**	[mesin peŋgiliŋ kopi]

| kettle | **cerek** | [tʃereʔ] |
| teapot | **teko** | [teko] |

lid	**tutup**	[tutup]
tea strainer	**saringan teh**	[sariŋan teh]
spoon	**sendok**	[sendoʔ]
teaspoon	**sendok teh**	[sendoʔ teh]
soup spoon	**sendok makan**	[sendoʔ makan]
fork	**garpu**	[garpu]
knife	**pisau**	[pisau]
tableware (dishes)	**piring mangkuk**	[piriŋ maŋkuʔ]
plate (dinner ~)	**piring**	[piriŋ]
saucer	**alas cangkir**	[alas ʧaŋkir]
shot glass	**seloki**	[seloki]
glass (tumbler)	**gelas**	[gelas]
cup	**cangkir**	[ʧaŋkir]
sugar bowl	**wadah gula**	[wadah gula]
salt shaker	**wadah garam**	[wadah garam]
pepper shaker	**wadah merica**	[wadah meriʧa]
butter dish	**wadah mentega**	[wadah mentega]
stock pot (soup pot)	**panci**	[panʧi]
frying pan (skillet)	**kuali**	[kuali]
ladle	**sudu**	[sudu]
colander	**saringan**	[sariŋan]
tray (serving ~)	**talam**	[talam]
bottle	**botol**	[botol]
jar (glass)	**gelas**	[gelas]
can	**kaleng**	[kaleŋ]
bottle opener	**pembuka botol**	[pembuka botol]
can opener	**pembuka kaleng**	[pembuka kaleŋ]
corkscrew	**kotrek**	[kotreʔ]
filter	**saringan**	[sariŋan]
to filter (vt)	**saringan**	[sariŋan]
trash, garbage (food waste, etc.)	**sampah**	[sampah]
trash can (kitchen ~)	**tong sampah**	[toŋ sampah]

72. Bathroom

bathroom	**kamar mandi**	[kamar mandi]
water	**air**	[air]
faucet	**keran**	[keran]
hot water	**air panas**	[air panas]
cold water	**air dingin**	[air diŋin]
toothpaste	**pasta gigi**	[pasta gigi]

| to brush one's teeth | menggosok gigi | [məŋgoso' gigi] |
| toothbrush | sikat gigi | [sikat gigi] |

to shave (vi)	bercukur	[bərtʃukur]
shaving foam	busa cukur	[busa tʃukur]
razor	pisau cukur	[pisau tʃukur]

to wash (one's hands, etc.)	mencuci	[məntʃutʃi]
to take a bath	mandi	[mandi]
shower	pancuran	[pantʃuran]
to take a shower	mandi pancuran	[mandi pantʃuran]

bathtub	bak mandi	[ba' mandi]
toilet (toilet bowl)	kloset	[kloset]
sink (washbasin)	wastafel	[wastafel]

| soap | sabun | [sabun] |
| soap dish | wadah sabun | [wadah sabun] |

sponge	spons	[spons]
shampoo	sampo	[sampo]
towel	handuk	[handu']
bathrobe	jubah mandi	[dʒʲubah mandi]

laundry (process)	pencucian	[pentʃutʃian]
washing machine	mesin cuci	[mesin tʃutʃi]
to do the laundry	mencuci	[məntʃutʃi]
laundry detergent	deterjen cuci	[deterdʒʲen tʃutʃi]

73. Household appliances

TV set	pesawat TV	[pesawat ti-vi]
tape recorder	alat perekam	[alat perekam]
VCR (video recorder)	video, VCR	[vidio], [vi-si-er]
radio	radio	[radio]
player (CD, MP3, etc.)	pemutar	[pemutar]

video projector	proyektor video	[proektor video]
home movie theater	bioskop rumah	[bioskop rumah]
DVD player	pemutar DVD	[pemutar di-vi-di]
amplifier	penguat	[peŋuat]
video game console	konsol permainan video	[konsol permajnan video]

video camera	kamera video	[kamera video]
camera (photo)	kamera	[kamera]
digital camera	kamera digital	[kamera digital]

vacuum cleaner	pengisap debu	[peɲisap debu]
iron (e.g., steam ~)	setrika	[setrika]
ironing board	papan setrika	[papan setrika]

telephone	**telepon**	[telepon]
cell phone	**ponsel**	[ponsel]
typewriter	**mesin ketik**	[mesin ketiʔ]
sewing machine	**mesin jahit**	[mesin dʒʲahit]
microphone	**mikrofon**	[mikrofon]
headphones	**headphone, fonkepala**	[headphone], [fonkepala]
remote control (TV)	**panel kendali**	[panel kendali]
CD, compact disc	**cakram kompak**	[tʃakram kompaʔ]
cassette, tape	**kaset**	[kaset]
vinyl record	**piringan hitam**	[piriŋan hitam]

THE EARTH. WEATHER

74. Outer space

space	**angkasa**	[aŋkasa]
space (as adj)	**angkasa**	[aŋkasa]
outer space	**ruang angkasa**	[ruaŋ aŋkasa]
world	**dunia**	[dunia]
universe	**jagat raya**	[dʒⁱagat raja]
galaxy	**galaksi**	[galaksi]
star	**bintang**	[bintaŋ]
constellation	**gugusan bintang**	[gugusan bintaŋ]
planet	**planet**	[planet]
satellite	**satelit**	[satelit]
meteorite	**meteorit**	[meteorit]
comet	**komet**	[komet]
asteroid	**asteroid**	[asteroid]
orbit	**orbit**	[orbit]
to revolve	**berputar**	[berputar]
(~ around the Earth)		
atmosphere	**atmosfer**	[atmosfer]
the Sun	**matahari**	[matahari]
solar system	**tata surya**	[tata surja]
solar eclipse	**gerhana matahari**	[gerhana matahari]
the Earth	**Bumi**	[bumi]
the Moon	**Bulan**	[bulan]
Mars	**Mars**	[mars]
Venus	**Venus**	[venus]
Jupiter	**Yupiter**	[yupiter]
Saturn	**Saturnus**	[saturnus]
Mercury	**Merkurius**	[merkurius]
Uranus	**Uranus**	[uranus]
Neptune	**Neptunus**	[neptunus]
Pluto	**Pluto**	[pluto]
Milky Way	**Bimasakti**	[bimasakti]
Great Bear (Ursa Major)	**Ursa Major**	[ursa madʒor]
North Star	**Bintang Utara**	[bintaŋ utara]
Martian	**makhluk Mars**	[mahluʔ mars]

extraterrestrial (n)	makhluk ruang angkasa	[mahluʔ ruaŋ aŋkasa]
alien	alien, makhluk asing	[alien], [mahluʔ asiŋ]
flying saucer	piring terbang	[piriŋ tərban]

spaceship	kapal antariksa	[kapal antariksa]
space station	stasiun antariksa	[stasiun antariksa]
blast-off	peluncuran	[peluntʃuran]

engine	mesin	[mesin]
nozzle	nosel	[nosel]
fuel	bahan bakar	[bahan bakar]

cockpit, flight deck	kokpit	[kokpit]
antenna	antena	[antena]
porthole	jendela	[dʒˈendela]
solar panel	sel surya	[sel surja]
spacesuit	pakaian antariksa	[pakajan antariksa]

| weightlessness | keadaan tanpa bobot | [keadaʔan tanpa bobot] |
| oxygen | oksigen | [oksigen] |

| docking (in space) | penggabungan | [peŋgabuŋan] |
| to dock (vi, vt) | bergabung | [bərgabuŋ] |

observatory	observatorium	[observatorium]
telescope	teleskop	[teleskop]
to observe (vt)	mengamati	[məŋamati]
to explore (vt)	mengeksplorasi	[məŋeksplorasi]

75. The Earth

the Earth	Bumi	[bumi]
the globe (the Earth)	bola Bumi	[bola bumi]
planet	planet	[planet]

atmosphere	atmosfer	[atmosfer]
geography	geografi	[geografi]
nature	alam	[alam]

globe (table ~)	globe	[globe]
map	peta	[peta]
atlas	atlas	[atlas]

Europe	Eropa	[eropa]
Asia	Asia	[asia]
Africa	Afrika	[afrika]
Australia	Australia	[australia]

| America | Amerika | [amerika] |
| North America | Amerika Utara | [amerika utara] |

South America	Amerika Selatan	[amerika selatan]
Antarctica	Antartika	[antartika]
the Arctic	Arktika	[arktika]

76. Cardinal directions

north	utara	[utara]
to the north	ke utara	[ke utara]
in the north	di utara	[di utara]
northern (adj)	utara	[utara]

south	selatan	[selatan]
to the south	ke selatan	[ke selatan]
in the south	di selatan	[di selatan]
southern (adj)	selatan	[selatan]

west	barat	[barat]
to the west	ke barat	[ke barat]
in the west	di barat	[di barat]
western (adj)	barat	[barat]

east	timur	[timur]
to the east	ke timur	[ke timur]
in the east	di timur	[di timur]
eastern (adj)	timur	[timur]

77. Sea. Ocean

sea	laut	[laut]
ocean	samudra	[samudra]
gulf (bay)	teluk	[teluʔ]
straits	selat	[selat]

| land (solid ground) | daratan | [daratan] |
| continent (mainland) | benua | [benua] |

island	pulau	[pulau]
peninsula	semenanjung, jazirah	[semenandʒⁱuŋ], [dʒⁱazirah]
archipelago	kepulauan	[kepulauan]

bay, cove	teluk	[teluʔ]
harbor	pelabuhan	[pelabuhan]
lagoon	laguna	[laguna]
cape	tanjung	[tandʒⁱuŋ]

atoll	pulau karang	[pulau karaŋ]
reef	terumbu	[terumbu]
coral	karang	[karaŋ]

coral reef	**terumbu karang**	[tərumbu karaŋ]
deep (adj)	**dalam**	[dalam]
depth (deep water)	**kedalaman**	[kedalaman]
abyss	**jurang**	[dʒʲuraŋ]
trench (e.g., Mariana ~)	**palung**	[paluŋ]
current (Ocean ~)	**arus**	[arus]
to surround (bathe)	**berbatasan dengan**	[bərbatasan deŋan]
shore	**pantai**	[pantaj]
coast	**pantai**	[pantaj]
flow (flood tide)	**air pasang**	[air pasaŋ]
ebb (ebb tide)	**air surut**	[air surut]
shoal	**beting**	[betiŋ]
bottom (~ of the sea)	**dasar**	[dasar]
wave	**gelombang**	[gelombaŋ]
crest (~ of a wave)	**puncak gelombang**	[puntʃaʔ gelombaŋ]
spume (sea foam)	**busa, buih**	[busa], [buih]
storm (sea storm)	**badai**	[badaj]
hurricane	**topan**	[topan]
tsunami	**tsunami**	[tsunami]
calm (dead ~)	**angin tenang**	[aŋin tenaŋ]
quiet, calm (adj)	**tenang**	[tenaŋ]
pole	**kutub**	[kutub]
polar (adj)	**kutub**	[kutub]
latitude	**lintang**	[lintaŋ]
longitude	**garis bujur**	[garis budʒʲur]
parallel	**sejajar**	[sedʒʲadʒʲar]
equator	**khatulistiwa**	[hatulistiwa]
sky	**langit**	[laŋit]
horizon	**horizon**	[horizon]
air	**udara**	[udara]
lighthouse	**mercusuar**	[mertʃusuar]
to dive (vi)	**menyelam**	[mənjelam]
to sink (ab. boat)	**karam**	[karam]
treasures	**harta karun**	[harta karun]

78. Seas' and Oceans' names

Atlantic Ocean	**Samudra Atlantik**	[samudra atlantiʔ]
Indian Ocean	**Samudra Hindia**	[samudra hindia]
Pacific Ocean	**Samudra Pasifik**	[samudra pasifiʔ]
Arctic Ocean	**Samudra Arktik**	[samudra arktiʔ]

Black Sea	**Laut Hitam**	[laut hitam]
Red Sea	**Laut Merah**	[laut merah]
Yellow Sea	**Laut Kuning**	[laut kuniŋ]
White Sea	**Laut Putih**	[laut putih]
Caspian Sea	**Laut Kaspia**	[laut kaspia]
Dead Sea	**Laut Mati**	[laut mati]
Mediterranean Sea	**Laut Tengah**	[laut teŋah]
Aegean Sea	**Laut Aegean**	[laut aegean]
Adriatic Sea	**Laut Adriatik**	[laut adriatiʔ]
Arabian Sea	**Laut Arab**	[laut arab]
Sea of Japan	**Laut Jepang**	[laut dʒˈepaŋ]
Bering Sea	**Laut Bering**	[laut beriŋ]
South China Sea	**Laut Cina Selatan**	[laut tʃina selatan]
Coral Sea	**Laut Karang**	[laut karaŋ]
Tasman Sea	**Laut Tasmania**	[laut tasmania]
Caribbean Sea	**Laut Karibia**	[laut karibia]
Barents Sea	**Laut Barents**	[laut barents]
Kara Sea	**Laut Kara**	[laut kara]
North Sea	**Laut Utara**	[laut utara]
Baltic Sea	**Laut Baltik**	[laut baltiʔ]
Norwegian Sea	**Laut Norwegia**	[laut norwegia]

79. Mountains

mountain	**gunung**	[gunuŋ]
mountain range	**jajaran gunung**	[dʒˈadʒˈaran gunuŋ]
mountain ridge	**sisir gunung**	[sisir gunuŋ]
summit, top	**puncak**	[puntʃaʔ]
peak	**puncak**	[puntʃaʔ]
foot (~ of the mountain)	**kaki**	[kaki]
slope (mountainside)	**lereng**	[lereŋ]
volcano	**gunung api**	[gunuŋ api]
active volcano	**gunung api yang aktif**	[gunuŋ api yaŋ aktif]
dormant volcano	**gunung api yang tidak aktif**	[gunuŋ api yaŋ tidaʔ aktif]
eruption	**erupsi, letusan**	[erupsi], [letusan]
crater	**kawah**	[kawah]
magma	**magma**	[magma]
lava	**lava, lahar**	[lava], [lahar]
molten (~ lava)	**pijar**	[pidʒˈar]
canyon	**kanyon**	[kanjon]

gorge	**jurang**	[dʒˈuraŋ]
crevice	**celah**	[ʧelah]
abyss (chasm)	**jurang**	[dʒˈuraŋ]
pass, col	**pass, celah**	[pass], [ʧelah]
plateau	**plato, dataran tinggi**	[plato], [dataran tiŋgi]
cliff	**tebing**	[tebiŋ]
hill	**bukit**	[bukit]
glacier	**gletser**	[gletser]
waterfall	**air terjun**	[air tərdʒˈun]
geyser	**geiser**	[geyser]
lake	**danau**	[danau]
plain	**dataran**	[dataran]
landscape	**landskap**	[landskap]
echo	**gema**	[gema]
alpinist	**pendaki gunung**	[pendaki gunuŋ]
rock climber	**pemanjat tebing**	[pemandʒˈat tebiŋ]
to conquer (in climbing)	**menaklukkan**	[mənakluʔkan]
climb (an easy ~)	**pendakian**	[pendakian]

80. Mountains names

The Alps	**Alpen**	[alpen]
Mont Blanc	**Mont Blanc**	[mon blan]
The Pyrenees	**Pirenia**	[pirenia]
The Carpathians	**Pegunungan Karpatia**	[pegunuŋan karpatia]
The Ural Mountains	**Pegunungan Ural**	[pegunuŋan ural]
The Caucasus Mountains	**Kaukasus**	[kaukasus]
Mount Elbrus	**Elbrus**	[elbrus]
The Altai Mountains	**Altai**	[altaj]
The Tian Shan	**Tien Shan**	[tjen ʃan]
The Pamir Mountains	**Pegunungan Pamir**	[pegunuŋan pamir]
The Himalayas	**Himalaya**	[himalaja]
Mount Everest	**Everest**	[everest]
The Andes	**Andes**	[andes]
Mount Kilimanjaro	**Kilimanjaro**	[kilimandʒˈaro]

81. Rivers

river	**sungai**	[suŋaj]
spring (natural source)	**mata air**	[mata air]
riverbed (river channel)	**badan sungai**	[badan suŋaj]

| basin (river valley) | **basin** | [basin] |
| to flow into … | **mengalir ke …** | [məŋalir ke …] |

| tributary | **anak sungai** | [ana' suŋaj] |
| bank (of river) | **tebing sungai** | [tebiŋ suŋaj] |

current (stream)	**arus**	[arus]
downstream (adv)	**ke hilir**	[ke hilir]
upstream (adv)	**ke hulu**	[ke hulu]

inundation	**banjir**	[bandʒir]
flooding	**banjir**	[bandʒir]
to overflow (vi)	**membanjiri**	[membandʒiri]
to flood (vt)	**membanjiri**	[membandʒiri]

| shallow (shoal) | **beting** | [betiŋ] |
| rapids | **jeram** | [dʒieram] |

dam	**dam, bendungan**	[dam], [benduŋan]
canal	**kanal, terusan**	[kanal], [tərusan]
reservoir (artificial lake)	**waduk**	[wadu']
sluice, lock	**pintu air**	[pintu air]

water body (pond, etc.)	**kolam**	[kolam]
swamp (marshland)	**rawa**	[rawa]
bog, marsh	**bencah, paya**	[bentʃah], [paja]
whirlpool	**pusaran air**	[pusaran air]

stream (brook)	**selokan**	[selokan]
drinking (ab. water)	**minum**	[minum]
fresh (~ water)	**tawar**	[tawar]

ice	**es**	[es]
to freeze over	**membeku**	[membeku]
(ab. river, etc.)		

82. Rivers' names

| Seine | **Seine** | [seine] |
| Loire | **Loire** | [loire] |

Thames	**Thames**	[tems]
Rhine	**Rein**	[reyn]
Danube	**Donau**	[donau]

Volga	**Volga**	[volga]
Don	**Don**	[don]
Lena	**Lena**	[lena]
Yellow River	**Suang Kuning**	[suaŋ kuniŋ]
Yangtze	**Yangtze**	[yaŋtze]

Mekong	**Mekong**	[mekoŋ]
Ganges	**Gangga**	[gaŋga]
Nile River	**Sungai Nil**	[suŋaj nil]
Congo River	**Kongo**	[koŋo]
Okavango River	**Okavango**	[okavaŋo]
Zambezi River	**Zambezi**	[zambezi]
Limpopo River	**Limpopo**	[limpopo]
Mississippi River	**Mississippi**	[misisipi]

83. Forest

forest, wood	**hutan**	[hutan]
forest (as adj)	**hutan**	[hutan]
thick forest	**hutan lebat**	[hutan lebat]
grove	**hutan kecil**	[hutan ketʃil]
forest clearing	**pembukaan hutan**	[pembuka'an hutan]
thicket	**semak belukar**	[sema' belukar]
scrubland	**belukar**	[belukar]
footpath (troddenpath)	**jalan setapak**	[dʒʲalan setapa']
gully	**parit**	[parit]
tree	**pohon**	[pohon]
leaf	**daun**	[daun]
leaves (foliage)	**daun-daunan**	[daun-daunan]
fall of leaves	**daun berguguran**	[daun berguguran]
to fall (ab. leaves)	**luruh**	[luruh]
top (of the tree)	**puncak**	[puntʃa']
branch	**cabang**	[tʃabaŋ]
bough	**dahan**	[dahan]
bud (on shrub, tree)	**tunas**	[tunas]
needle (of pine tree)	**daun jarum**	[daun dʒʲarum]
pine cone	**buah pinus**	[buah pinus]
hollow (in a tree)	**lubang pohon**	[lubaŋ pohon]
nest	**sarang**	[saraŋ]
burrow (animal hole)	**lubang**	[lubaŋ]
trunk	**batang**	[bataŋ]
root	**akar**	[akar]
bark	**kulit**	[kulit]
moss	**lumut**	[lumut]
to uproot (remove trees or tree stumps)	**mencabut**	[mentʃabut]
to chop down	**menebang**	[menebaŋ]

to deforest (vt)	deforestasi, penggundulan hutan	[deforestasi], [pengundulan hutan]
tree stump	tunggul	[tuŋgul]
campfire	api unggun	[api uŋgun]
forest fire	kebakaran hutan	[kebakaran hutan]
to extinguish (vt)	memadamkan	[memadamkan]
forest ranger	penjaga hutan	[penʤaga hutan]
protection	perlindungan	[pərlinduŋan]
to protect (~ nature)	melindungi	[melinduŋi]
poacher	pemburu ilegal	[pemburu ilegal]
steel trap	perangkap	[pəraŋkap]
to gather, to pick (vt)	memetik	[memetiʔ]
to lose one's way	tersesat	[tərsesat]

84. Natural resources

natural resources	sumber daya alam	[sumber daja alam]
minerals	bahan tambang	[bahan tambaŋ]
deposits	endapan	[endapan]
field (e.g., oilfield)	ladang	[ladaŋ]
to mine (extract)	menambang	[mənambaŋ]
mining (extraction)	pertambangan	[pərtambaŋan]
ore	bijih	[biʤih]
mine (e.g., for coal)	tambang	[tambaŋ]
shaft (mine ~)	sumur tambang	[sumur tambaŋ]
miner	penambang	[penambaŋ]
gas (natural ~)	gas	[gas]
gas pipeline	pipa saluran gas	[pipa saluran gas]
oil (petroleum)	petroleum, minyak	[petroleum], [minjaʔ]
oil pipeline	pipa saluran minyak	[pipa saluran minjaʔ]
oil well	sumur minyak	[sumur minjaʔ]
derrick (tower)	menara bor minyak	[mənara bor minjaʔ]
tanker	kapal tangki	[kapal taŋki]
sand	pasir	[pasir]
limestone	batu kapur	[batu kapur]
gravel	kerikil	[kerikil]
peat	gambut	[gambut]
clay	tanah liat	[tanah liat]
coal	arang	[araŋ]
iron (ore)	besi	[besi]
gold	emas	[emas]
silver	perak	[peraʔ]

nickel	nikel	[nikel]
copper	tembaga	[tembaga]
zinc	seng	[seŋ]
manganese	mangan	[maŋan]
mercury	air raksa	[air raksa]
lead	timbal	[timbal]
mineral	mineral	[mineral]
crystal	kristal, hablur	[kristal], [hablur]
marble	marmer	[marmer]
uranium	uranium	[uranium]

85. Weather

weather	cuaca	[tʃuatʃa]
weather forecast	prakiraan cuaca	[prakira'an tʃuatʃa]
temperature	temperatur, suhu	[temperatur], [suhu]
thermometer	termometer	[termometər]
barometer	barometer	[barometer]
humid (adj)	lembap	[lembap]
humidity	kelembapan	[kelembapan]
heat (extreme ~)	panas, gerah	[panas], [gerah]
hot (torrid)	panas terik	[panas teriʔ]
it's hot	panas	[panas]
it's warm	hangat	[haŋat]
warm (moderately hot)	hangat	[haŋat]
it's cold	dingin	[diŋin]
cold (adj)	dingin	[diŋin]
sun	matahari	[matahari]
to shine (vi)	bersinar	[bersinar]
sunny (day)	cerah	[tʃerah]
to come up (vi)	terbit	[terbit]
to set (vi)	terbenam	[terbenam]
cloud	awan	[awan]
cloudy (adj)	berawan	[berawan]
rain cloud	awan mendung	[awan menduŋ]
somber (gloomy)	mendung	[menduŋ]
rain	hujan	[hudʒian]
it's raining	hujan turun	[hudʒian turun]
rainy (~ day, weather)	hujan	[hudʒian]
to drizzle (vi)	gerimis	[gerimis]
pouring rain	hujan lebat	[hudʒian lebat]

downpour	hujan lebat	[huʤan lebat]
heavy (e.g., ~ rain)	lebat	[lebat]
puddle	kubangan	[kubaŋan]
to get wet (in rain)	kehujanan	[kehuʤʲanan]

fog (mist)	kabut	[kabut]
foggy	berkabut	[bərkabut]
snow	salju	[salʤʲu]
it's snowing	turun salju	[turun salʤʲu]

86. Severe weather. Natural disasters

thunderstorm	hujan badai	[huʤan badaj]
lightning (~ strike)	kilat	[kilat]
to flash (vi)	berkilau	[bərkilau]

thunder	petir	[petir]
to thunder (vi)	bergemuruh	[bergemuruh]
it's thundering	bergemuruh	[bergemuruh]

| hail | hujan es | [huʤan es] |
| it's hailing | hujan es | [huʤan es] |

| to flood (vt) | membanjiri | [membanʤiri] |
| flood, inundation | banjir | [banʤir] |

earthquake	gempa bumi	[gempa bumi]
tremor, quake	gempa	[gempa]
epicenter	episentrum	[episentrum]

| eruption | erupsi, letusan | [erupsi], [letusan] |
| lava | lava, lahar | [lava], [lahar] |

twister	puting beliung	[putiŋ beliuŋ]
tornado	tornado	[tornado]
typhoon	topan	[topan]

hurricane	topan	[topan]
storm	badai	[badaj]
tsunami	tsunami	[tsunami]

cyclone	siklon	[siklon]
bad weather	cuaca buruk	[ʧuaʧa buruʔ]
fire (accident)	kebakaran	[kebakaran]
disaster	bencana	[benʧana]
meteorite	meteorit	[meteorit]

avalanche	longsor	[loŋsor]
snowslide	salju longsor	[salʤʲu loŋsor]
blizzard	badai salju	[badaj salʤʲu]

| snowstorm | **badai salju** | [badaj saldʒʲu] |

FAUNA

87. Mammals. Predators

predator	**predator, pemangsa**	[predator], [pemaŋsa]
tiger	**harimau**	[harimau]
lion	**singa**	[siŋa]
wolf	**serigala**	[serigala]
fox	**rubah**	[rubah]
jaguar	**jaguar**	[ʤaguar]
leopard	**leopard, macan tutul**	[leopard], [matʃan tutul]
cheetah	**cheetah**	[ʧeetah]
black panther	**harimau kumbang**	[harimau kumbaŋ]
puma	**singa gunung**	[siŋa gunuŋ]
snow leopard	**harimau bintang salju**	[harimau bintaŋ salʤʲu]
lynx	**lynx**	[links]
coyote	**koyote**	[koyot]
jackal	**jakal**	[ʤʲakal]
hyena	**hiena**	[hiena]

88. Wild animals

animal	**binatang**	[binataŋ]
beast (animal)	**binatang buas**	[binataŋ buas]
squirrel	**bajing**	[baʤiŋ]
hedgehog	**landak susu**	[landa' susu]
hare	**terwelu**	[tərwelu]
rabbit	**kelinci**	[kelinʧi]
badger	**luak**	[lua']
raccoon	**rakun**	[rakun]
hamster	**hamster**	[hamster]
marmot	**marmut**	[marmut]
mole	**tikus mondok**	[tikus mondo']
mouse	**tikus**	[tikus]
rat	**tikus besar**	[tikus besar]
bat	**kelelawar**	[kelelawar]
ermine	**ermin**	[ermin]
sable	**sabel**	[sabel]

marten	**marten**	[marten]
weasel	**musang**	[musaŋ]
mink	**cerpelai**	[tʃerpelaj]
beaver	**beaver**	[beaver]
otter	**berang-berang**	[bəraŋ-bəraŋ]
horse	**kuda**	[kuda]
moose	**rusa besar**	[rusa besar]
deer	**rusa**	[rusa]
camel	**unta**	[unta]
bison	**bison**	[bison]
aurochs	**aurochs**	[oroks]
buffalo	**kerbau**	[kerbau]
zebra	**kuda belang**	[kuda belaŋ]
antelope	**antelop**	[antelop]
roe deer	**kijang**	[kidʒʲaŋ]
fallow deer	**rusa**	[rusa]
chamois	**chamois**	[ʃemva]
wild boar	**babi hutan jantan**	[babi hutan dʒʲantan]
whale	**ikan paus**	[ikan paus]
seal	**anjing laut**	[andʒiŋ laut]
walrus	**walrus**	[walrus]
fur seal	**anjing laut berbulu**	[andʒiŋ laut bərbulu]
dolphin	**lumba-lumba**	[lumba-lumba]
bear	**beruang**	[bəruaŋ]
polar bear	**beruang kutub**	[bəruaŋ kutub]
panda	**panda**	[panda]
monkey	**monyet**	[monjet]
chimpanzee	**simpanse**	[simpanse]
orangutan	**orang utan**	[oraŋ utan]
gorilla	**gorila**	[gorila]
macaque	**kera**	[kera]
gibbon	**siamang, ungka**	[siamaŋ], [uŋka]
elephant	**gajah**	[gadʒʲah]
rhinoceros	**badak**	[badaʔ]
giraffe	**jerapah**	[dʒʲerapah]
hippopotamus	**kuda nil**	[kuda nil]
kangaroo	**kanguru**	[kaŋuru]
koala (bear)	**koala**	[koala]
mongoose	**garangan**	[garaŋan]
chinchilla	**chinchilla**	[tʃintʃilla]
skunk	**sigung**	[siguŋ]
porcupine	**landak**	[landaʔ]

89. Domestic animals

cat	kucing betina	[kutʃiŋ betina]
tomcat	kucing jantan	[kutʃiŋ dʒʲantan]
dog	anjing	[andʒiŋ]

horse	kuda	[kuda]
stallion (male horse)	kuda jantan	[kuda dʒʲantan]
mare	kuda betina	[kuda betina]

cow	sapi	[sapi]
bull	sapi jantan	[sapi dʒʲantan]
ox	lembu jantan	[lembu dʒʲantan]

sheep (ewe)	domba	[domba]
ram	domba jantan	[domba dʒʲantan]
goat	kambing betina	[kambiŋ betina]
billy goat, he-goat	kambing jantan	[kambiŋ dʒʲantan]

| donkey | keledai | [keledaj] |
| mule | bagal | [bagal] |

pig, hog	babi	[babi]
piglet	anak babi	[anaʔ babi]
rabbit	kelinci	[kelintʃi]

| hen (chicken) | ayam betina | [ajam betina] |
| rooster | ayam jago | [ajam dʒʲago] |

duck	bebek	[bebeʔ]
drake	bebek jantan	[bebeʔ dʒʲantan]
goose	angsa	[aŋsa]

| tom turkey, gobbler | kalkun jantan | [kalkun dʒʲantan] |
| turkey (hen) | kalkun betina | [kalkun betina] |

domestic animals	binatang piaraan	[binataŋ piaraʔan]
tame (e.g., ~ hamster)	jinak	[dʒinaʔ]
to tame (vt)	menjinakkan	[mendʒinaʔkan]
to breed (vt)	membiakkan	[membiaʔkan]

farm	peternakan	[peternakan]
poultry	unggas	[uŋgas]
cattle	ternak	[ternaʔ]
herd (cattle)	kawanan	[kawanan]

stable	kandang kuda	[kandaŋ kuda]
pigpen	kandang babi	[kandaŋ babi]
cowshed	kandang sapi	[kandaŋ sapi]
rabbit hutch	sangkar kelinci	[saŋkar kelintʃi]
hen house	kandang ayam	[kandaŋ ajam]

90. Birds

bird	**burung**	[buruŋ]
pigeon	**burung dara**	[buruŋ dara]
sparrow	**burung gereja**	[buruŋ geredʒ'a]
tit (great tit)	**burung tit**	[buruŋ tit]
magpie	**burung murai**	[buruŋ muraj]
raven	**burung raven**	[buruŋ raven]
crow	**burung gagak**	[buruŋ gaga']
jackdaw	**burung gagak kecil**	[buruŋ gaga' ketʃil]
rook	**burung rook**	[buruŋ roo']
duck	**bebek**	[bebe']
goose	**angsa**	[aŋsa]
pheasant	**burung kuau**	[buruŋ kuau]
eagle	**rajawali**	[radʒ'awali]
hawk	**elang**	[elaŋ]
falcon	**alap-alap**	[alap-alap]
vulture	**hering**	[heriŋ]
condor (Andean ~)	**kondor**	[kondor]
swan	**angsa**	[aŋsa]
crane	**burung jenjang**	[buruŋ dʒ'endʒ'aŋ]
stork	**bangau**	[baŋau]
parrot	**burung nuri**	[buruŋ nuri]
hummingbird	**burung kolibri**	[buruŋ kolibri]
peacock	**burung merak**	[buruŋ mera']
ostrich	**burung unta**	[buruŋ unta]
heron	**kuntul**	[kuntul]
flamingo	**burung flamingo**	[buruŋ flamiŋo]
pelican	**pelikan**	[pelikan]
nightingale	**burung bulbul**	[buruŋ bulbul]
swallow	**burung walet**	[buruŋ walet]
thrush	**burung jalak**	[buruŋ dʒ'ala']
song thrush	**burung jalak suren**	[buruŋ dʒ'ala' suren]
blackbird	**burung jalak hitam**	[buruŋ dʒ'ala' hitam]
swift	**burung apus-apus**	[buruŋ apus-apus]
lark	**burung lark**	[buruŋ lar']
quail	**burung puyuh**	[buruŋ puyuh]
woodpecker	**burung pelatuk**	[buruŋ pelatu']
cuckoo	**burung kukuk**	[buruŋ kuku']
owl	**burung hantu**	[buruŋ hantu]
eagle owl	**burung hantu bertanduk**	[buruŋ hantu bertandu']

wood grouse	burung murai kayu	[buruŋ muraj kaju]
black grouse	burung belibis hitam	[buruŋ belibis hitam]
partridge	ayam hutan	[ajam hutan]
starling	burung starling	[buruŋ starliŋ]
canary	burung kenari	[buruŋ kenari]
hazel grouse	ayam hutan hazel	[ajam hutan hazel]
chaffinch	burung chaffinch	[buruŋ tʃaffintʃ]
bullfinch	burung bullfinch	[buruŋ bullfintʃ]
seagull	burung camar	[buruŋ tʃamar]
albatross	albatros	[albatros]
penguin	penguin	[peŋuin]

91. Fish. Marine animals

bream	ikan bream	[ikan bream]
carp	ikan karper	[ikan karper]
perch	ikan tilapia	[ikan tilapia]
catfish	lais junggang	[lajs dʒˈuŋgaŋ]
pike	ikan pike	[ikan paik]
salmon	salmon	[salmon]
sturgeon	ikan sturgeon	[ikan sturdʒˈen]
herring	ikan haring	[ikan hariŋ]
Atlantic salmon	ikan salem	[ikan salem]
mackerel	ikan kembung	[ikan kembuŋ]
flatfish	ikan sebelah	[ikan sebelah]
zander, pike perch	ikan seligi tenggeran	[ikan seligi teŋgeran]
cod	ikan kod	[ikan kod]
tuna	tuna	[tuna]
trout	ikan forel	[ikan forel]
eel	belut	[belut]
electric ray	ikan pari listrik	[ikan pari listriʔ]
moray eel	belut moray	[belut morey]
piranha	ikan piranha	[ikan piranha]
shark	ikan hiu	[ikan hiu]
dolphin	lumba-lumba	[lumba-lumba]
whale	ikan paus	[ikan paus]
crab	kepiting	[kepitiŋ]
jellyfish	ubur-ubur	[ubur-ubur]
octopus	gurita	[gurita]
starfish	bintang laut	[bintaŋ laut]
sea urchin	landak laut	[landaʔ laut]

seahorse	kuda laut	[kuda laut]
oyster	tiram	[tiram]
shrimp	udang	[udaŋ]
lobster	udang karang	[udaŋ karaŋ]
spiny lobster	lobster berduri	[lobster bərduri]

92. Amphibians. Reptiles

snake	ular	[ular]
venomous (snake)	berbisa	[bərbisa]
viper	ular viper	[ular viper]
cobra	kobra	[kobra]
python	ular sanca	[ular santʃa]
boa	ular boa	[ular boa]
grass snake	ular tanah	[ular tanah]
rattle snake	ular derik	[ular deriʔ]
anaconda	ular anakonda	[ular anakonda]
lizard	kadal	[kadal]
iguana	iguana	[iguana]
monitor lizard	biawak	[biawaʔ]
salamander	salamander	[salamander]
chameleon	bunglon	[buŋlon]
scorpion	kalajengking	[kaladʒˈeŋkiŋ]
turtle	kura-kura	[kura-kura]
frog	katak	[kataʔ]
toad	kodok	[kodoʔ]
crocodile	buaya	[buaja]

93. Insects

insect, bug	serangga	[seraŋga]
butterfly	kupu-kupu	[kupu-kupu]
ant	semut	[semut]
fly	lalat	[lalat]
mosquito	nyamuk	[njamuʔ]
beetle	kumbang	[kumbaŋ]
wasp	tawon	[tawon]
bee	lebah	[lebah]
bumblebee	kumbang	[kumbaŋ]
gadfly (botfly)	lalat kerbau	[lalat kerbau]
spider	laba-laba	[laba-laba]
spiderweb	sarang laba-laba	[saraŋ laba-laba]

dragonfly	capung	[ʧapuŋ]
grasshopper	belalang	[belalaŋ]
moth (night butterfly)	ngengat	[ŋeŋat]
cockroach	kecoa	[keʧoa]
tick	kutu	[kutu]
flea	kutu loncat	[kutu lonʧat]
midge	agas	[agas]
locust	belalang	[belalaŋ]
snail	siput	[siput]
cricket	jangkrik	[ʤʲaŋkriʔ]
lightning bug	kunang-kunang	[kunaŋ-kunaŋ]
ladybug	kumbang koksi	[kumbaŋ koksi]
cockchafer	kumbang Cockchafer	[kumbaŋ kokʃafer]
leech	lintah	[lintah]
caterpillar	ulat	[ulat]
earthworm	cacing	[ʧatʃiŋ]
larva	larva	[larva]

FLORA

94. Trees

tree	**pohon**	[pohon]
deciduous (adj)	**daun luruh**	[daun luruh]
coniferous (adj)	**pohon jarum**	[pohon dʒarum]
evergreen (adj)	**selalu hijau**	[selalu hidʒau]
apple tree	**pohon apel**	[pohon apel]
pear tree	**pohon pir**	[pohon pir]
sweet cherry tree	**pohon ceri manis**	[pohon tʃeri manis]
sour cherry tree	**pohon ceri asam**	[pohon tʃeri asam]
plum tree	**pohon plum**	[pohon plum]
birch	**pohon berk**	[pohon bər']
oak	**pohon eik**	[pohon ei']
linden tree	**pohon linden**	[pohon linden]
aspen	**pohon aspen**	[pohon aspen]
maple	**pohon mapel**	[pohon mapel]
spruce	**pohon den**	[pohon den]
pine	**pohon pinus**	[pohon pinus]
larch	**pohon larch**	[pohon lartʃ]
fir tree	**pohon fir**	[pohon fir]
cedar	**pohon aras**	[pohon aras]
poplar	**pohon poplar**	[pohon poplar]
rowan	**pohon rowan**	[pohon rowan]
willow	**pohon dedalu**	[pohon dedalu]
alder	**pohon alder**	[pohon alder]
beech	**pohon nothofagus**	[pohon notofagus]
elm	**pohon elm**	[pohon elm]
ash (tree)	**pohon abu**	[pohon abu]
chestnut	**kastanye**	[kastanje]
magnolia	**magnolia**	[magnolia]
palm tree	**palem**	[palem]
cypress	**pokok cipres**	[poko' sipres]
mangrove	**bakau**	[bakau]
baobab	**baobab**	[baobab]
eucalyptus	**kayu putih**	[kaju putih]
sequoia	**sequoia**	[sekuoia]

95. Shrubs

bush	**rumpun**	[rumpun]
shrub	**semak**	[sema']
grapevine	**pohon anggur**	[pohon aŋgur]
vineyard	**kebun anggur**	[kebun aŋgur]
raspberry bush	**pohon frambus**	[pohon frambus]
blackcurrant bush	**pohon blackcurrant**	[pohon ble'karen]
redcurrant bush	**pohon redcurrant**	[pohon redkaren]
gooseberry bush	**pohon arbei hijau**	[pohon arbei hiʤʲau]
acacia	**pohon akasia**	[pohon akasia]
barberry	**pohon barberis**	[pohon barberis]
jasmine	**melati**	[melati]
juniper	**pohon juniper**	[pohon ʤʲuniper]
rosebush	**pohon mawar**	[pohon mawar]
dog rose	**pohon mawar liar**	[pohon mawar liar]

96. Fruits. Berries

fruit	**buah**	[buah]
fruits	**buah-buahan**	[buah-buahan]
apple	**apel**	[apel]
pear	**pir**	[pir]
plum	**plum**	[plum]
strawberry (garden ~)	**stroberi**	[stroberi]
sour cherry	**buah ceri asam**	[buah tʃeri asam]
sweet cherry	**buah ceri manis**	[buah tʃeri manis]
grape	**buah anggur**	[buah aŋgur]
raspberry	**buah frambus**	[buah frambus]
blackcurrant	**blackcurrant**	[ble'karen]
redcurrant	**redcurrant**	[redkaren]
gooseberry	**buah arbei hijau**	[buah arbei hiʤʲau]
cranberry	**buah kranberi**	[buah kranberi]
orange	**jeruk manis**	[ʤʲeru' manis]
mandarin	**jeruk mandarin**	[ʤʲeru' mandarin]
pineapple	**nanas**	[nanas]
banana	**pisang**	[pisaŋ]
date	**buah kurma**	[buah kurma]
lemon	**jeruk sitrun**	[ʤʲeru' sitrun]
apricot	**aprikot**	[aprikot]

peach	**persik**	[persiʔ]
kiwi	**kiwi**	[kiwi]
grapefruit	**jeruk Bali**	[dʒⁱeruʔ bali]
berry	**buah beri**	[buah bɛri]
berries	**buah-buah beri**	[buah-buah bɛri]
cowberry	**buah cowberry**	[buah kowbɛri]
wild strawberry	**stroberi liar**	[stroberi liar]
bilberry	**buah bilberi**	[buah bilbɛri]

97. Flowers. Plants

flower	**bunga**	[buŋa]
bouquet (of flowers)	**buket**	[buket]
rose (flower)	**mawar**	[mawar]
tulip	**tulip**	[tulip]
carnation	**bunga anyelir**	[buŋa anjelir]
gladiolus	**bunga gladiol**	[buŋa gladiol]
cornflower	**cornflower**	[kornflawa]
harebell	**bunga lonceng biru**	[buŋa lontʃeŋ biru]
dandelion	**dandelion**	[dandelion]
camomile	**bunga margrit**	[buŋa margrit]
aloe	**lidah buaya**	[lidah buaja]
cactus	**kaktus**	[kaktus]
rubber plant, ficus	**pohon ara**	[pohon ara]
lily	**bunga lili**	[buŋa lili]
geranium	**geranium**	[geranium]
hyacinth	**bunga bakung lembayung**	[buŋa bakuŋ lembajuŋ]
mimosa	**putri malu**	[putri malu]
narcissus	**bunga narsis**	[buŋa narsis]
nasturtium	**bunga nasturtium**	[buŋa nasturtium]
orchid	**anggrek**	[aŋgreʔ]
peony	**bunga peoni**	[buŋa peoni]
violet	**bunga violet**	[buŋa violet]
pansy	**bunga pansy**	[buŋa pansi]
forget-me-not	**bunga jangan-lupakan-daku**	[buŋa dʒⁱaŋan-lupakan-daku]
daisy	**bunga desi**	[buŋa desi]
poppy	**bunga madat**	[buŋa madat]
hemp	**rami**	[rami]
mint	**mint**	[min]

lily of the valley	lili lembah	[lili lembah]
snowdrop	bunga tetesan salju	[buŋa tetesan saldʒʲu]
nettle	jelatang	[dʒʲelataŋ]
sorrel	daun sorrel	[daun sorrel]
water lily	lili air	[lili air]
fern	pakis	[pakis]
lichen	lichen	[litʃen]
greenhouse (tropical ~)	rumah kaca	[rumah katʃa]
lawn	halaman berumput	[halaman berumput]
flowerbed	bedeng bunga	[bedeŋ buŋa]
plant	tumbuhan	[tumbuhan]
grass	rumput	[rumput]
blade of grass	sehelai rumput	[sehelaj rumput]
leaf	daun	[daun]
petal	kelopak	[kelopaʔ]
stem	batang	[bataŋ]
tuber	ubi	[ubi]
young plant (shoot)	tunas	[tunas]
thorn	duri	[duri]
to blossom (vi)	berbunga	[berbuŋa]
to fade, to wither	layu	[laju]
smell (odor)	bau	[bau]
to cut (flowers)	memotong	[memotoŋ]
to pick (a flower)	memetik	[memetiʔ]

98. Cereals, grains

grain	biji-bijian	[bidʒi-bidʒian]
cereal crops	padi-padian	[padi-padian]
ear (of barley, etc.)	bulir	[bulir]
wheat	gandum	[gandum]
rye	gandum hitam	[gandum hitam]
oats	oat	[oat]
millet	jawawut	[dʒʲawawut]
barley	jelai	[dʒʲelaj]
corn	jagung	[dʒʲaguŋ]
rice	beras	[beras]
buckwheat	buckwheat	[bakvit]
pea plant	kacang polong	[katʃaŋ poloŋ]
kidney bean	kacang buncis	[katʃaŋ buntʃis]
soy	kacang kedelai	[katʃaŋ kedelaj]

lentil	**kacang lentil**	[katʃaŋ lentil]
beans (pulse crops)	**kacang-kacangan**	[katʃaŋ-katʃaŋan]

COUNTRIES OF THE WORLD

99. Countries. Part 1

Afghanistan	**Afghanistan**	[afganistan]
Albania	**Albania**	[albania]
Argentina	**Argentina**	[argentina]
Armenia	**Armenia**	[armenia]
Australia	**Australia**	[australia]
Austria	**Austria**	[austria]
Azerbaijan	**Azerbaijan**	[azerbajdʒʲan]
The Bahamas	**Kepulauan Bahama**	[kepulauan bahama]
Bangladesh	**Bangladesh**	[baŋladeʃ]
Belarus	**Belarusia**	[belarusia]
Belgium	**Belgia**	[belgia]
Bolivia	**Bolivia**	[bolivia]
Bosnia and Herzegovina	**Bosnia-Hercegovina**	[bosnia-hersegovina]
Brazil	**Brasil**	[brasil]
Bulgaria	**Bulgaria**	[bulgaria]
Cambodia	**Kamboja**	[kambodʒʲa]
Canada	**Kanada**	[kanada]
Chile	**Chili**	[tʃili]
China	**Tiongkok**	[tjoŋkoʔ]
Colombia	**Kolombia**	[kolombia]
Croatia	**Kroasia**	[kroasia]
Cuba	**Kuba**	[kuba]
Cyprus	**Siprus**	[siprus]
Czech Republic	**Republik Ceko**	[republiʔ tʃeko]
Denmark	**Denmark**	[denmarʔ]
Dominican Republic	**Republik Dominika**	[republiʔ dominika]
Ecuador	**Ekuador**	[ekuador]
Egypt	**Mesir**	[mesir]
England	**Inggris**	[iŋgris]
Estonia	**Estonia**	[estonia]
Finland	**Finlandia**	[finlandia]
France	**Prancis**	[prantʃis]
French Polynesia	**Polinesia Prancis**	[polinesia prantʃis]
Georgia	**Georgia**	[dʒordʒia]
Germany	**Jerman**	[dʒʲerman]
Ghana	**Ghana**	[gana]
Great Britain	**Britania Raya**	[britania raja]
Greece	**Yunani**	[yunani]

| Haiti | **Haiti** | [haiti] |
| Hungary | **Hongaria** | [hoŋaria] |

100. Countries. Part 2

Iceland	**Islandia**	[islandia]
India	**India**	[india]
Indonesia	**Indonesia**	[indonesia]
Iran	**Iran**	[iran]
Iraq	**Irak**	[ira']
Ireland	**Irlandia**	[irlandia]
Israel	**Israel**	[israel]
Italy	**Italia**	[italia]

Jamaica	**Jamaika**	[dʒˈamajka]
Japan	**Jepang**	[dʒˈepaŋ]
Jordan	**Yordania**	[yordania]
Kazakhstan	**Kazakistan**	[kazakstan]
Kenya	**Kenya**	[kenia]
Kirghizia	**Kirgizia**	[kirgizia]
Kuwait	**Kuwait**	[kuweyt]

Laos	**Laos**	[laos]
Latvia	**Latvia**	[latvia]
Lebanon	**Lebanon**	[lebanon]
Libya	**Libia**	[libia]
Liechtenstein	**Liechtenstein**	[lajhtensteyn]
Lithuania	**Lituania**	[lituania]
Luxembourg	**Luksemburg**	[luksemburg]

Macedonia (Republic of ~)	**Makedonia**	[makedonia]
Madagascar	**Madagaskar**	[madagaskar]
Malaysia	**Malaysia**	[malajsia]
Malta	**Malta**	[malta]
Mexico	**Meksiko**	[meksiko]
Moldova, Moldavia	**Moldova**	[moldova]

Monaco	**Monako**	[monako]
Mongolia	**Mongolia**	[moŋolia]
Montenegro	**Montenegro**	[montenegro]

| Morocco | **Maroko** | [maroko] |
| Myanmar | **Myanmar** | [myanmar] |

Namibia	**Namibia**	[namibia]
Nepal	**Nepal**	[nepal]
Netherlands	**Belanda**	[belanda]
New Zealand	**Selandia Baru**	[selandia baru]
North Korea	**Korea Utara**	[korea utara]
Norway	**Norwegia**	[norwegia]

101. Countries. Part 3

Pakistan	**Pakistan**	[pakistan]
Palestine	**Palestina**	[palestina]
Panama	**Panama**	[panama]
Paraguay	**Paraguay**	[paraguaj]
Peru	**Peru**	[peru]
Poland	**Polandia**	[polandia]
Portugal	**Portugal**	[portugal]
Romania	**Romania**	[romania]
Russia	**Rusia**	[rusia]
Saudi Arabia	**Arab Saudi**	[arab saudi]
Scotland	**Skotlandia**	[skotlandia]
Senegal	**Senegal**	[senegal]
Serbia	**Serbia**	[serbia]
Slovakia	**Slowakia**	[slowakia]
Slovenia	**Slovenia**	[slovenia]
South Africa	**Afrika Selatan**	[afrika selatan]
South Korea	**Korea Selatan**	[korea selatan]
Spain	**Spanyol**	[spanjol]
Suriname	**Suriname**	[suriname]
Sweden	**Swedia**	[swedia]
Switzerland	**Swiss**	[swiss]
Syria	**Suriah**	[suriah]
Taiwan	**Taiwan**	[tajwan]
Tajikistan	**Tajikistan**	[tadʒikistan]
Tanzania	**Tanzania**	[tanzania]
Tasmania	**Tasmania**	[tasmania]
Thailand	**Thailand**	[tajland]
Tunisia	**Tunisia**	[tunisia]
Turkey	**Turki**	[turki]
Turkmenistan	**Turkmenistan**	[turkmenistan]
Ukraine	**Ukraina**	[ukrajna]
United Arab Emirates	**Uni Emirat Arab**	[uni emirat arab]
United States of America	**Amerika Serikat**	[amerika serikat]
Uruguay	**Uruguay**	[uruguaj]
Uzbekistan	**Uzbekistan**	[uzbekistan]
Vatican	**Vatikan**	[vatikan]
Venezuela	**Venezuela**	[venezuela]
Vietnam	**Vietnam**	[vjetnam]
Zanzibar	**Zanzibar**	[zanzibar]